The
Women
of
Easter

Other Books by Liz Curtis Higgs

Nonfiction
Bad Girls of the Bible
Really Bad Girls of the Bible
Unveiling Mary Magdalene
Slightly Bad Girls of the Bible
Rise and Shine
Embrace Grace
My Heart's in the Lowlands
The Girl's Still Got It
The Women of Christmas
It's Good to Be Queen
31 Verses to Write on Your Heart

Contemporary Fiction
Mixed Signals
Bookends
Mercy Like Sunlight

Historical Fiction
Thorn in My Heart
Fair Is the Rose
Whence Came a Prince
Grace in Thine Eyes
Here Burns My Candle
Mine Is the Night
A Wreath of Snow

Children's
The Parable of the Lily
The Sunflower Parable
The Pumpkin Patch Parable
The Pine Tree Parable
Parable Treasury

LIZ CURTIS HIGGS

The Women *of* Easter

Encounter the Savior with

MARY OF BETHANY, MARY OF NAZARETH,

and MARY MAGDALENE

WATERBROOK

THE WOMEN OF EASTER

All Scripture quotations, unless otherwise indicated, are taken from the Holy Bible, New International Version®, NIV®. Copyright © 1973, 1978, 1984, 2011 by Biblica Inc.® Used by permission. All rights reserved worldwide. For a list of the additional Bible versions that are quoted, see page 225.

Hardcover ISBN 978-1-60142-682-6
eBook ISBN 978-1-60142-683-3

Published in the United States by WaterBrook, an imprint of the Crown Publishing Group, a division of Penguin Random House LLC, New York.

WATERBROOK® and its deer colophon are registered trademarks of Penguin Random House LLC.

Library of Congress Cataloging-in-Publication Data
Names: Higgs, Liz Curtis, author.
Title: The women of Easter : encounter the Savior with Mary of Bethany, Mary of
    Nazareth, and Mary Magdalene / Liz Curtis Higgs.
Description: First Edition. | Colorado Springs, Colorado : WaterBrook, 2017. | Includes
    bibliographical references.
Identifiers: LCCN 2016044824 (print) | LCCN 2016046540 (ebook) | ISBN
    9781601426826 (hardcover) | ISBN 9781601426833 (electronic)
Subjects: LCSH: Women in the Bible. | Mary, of Bethany, Saint. | Mary, Blessed Virgin,
    Saint. | Mary Magdalene, Saint. | Jesus Christ—Friends and associates.
Classification: LCC BS2445 .H54 2017 (print) | LCC BS2445 (ebook) | DDC
    232.9/7082—dc23
LC record available at https://lccn.loc.gov/2016044824

Printed in the United States of America
2018

10 9 8 7 6

To my big sisters, Sarah Schwarz and Mary Dickinson,
remembering our Easter mornings together,
when we wore hats and gloves
and Mom-made dresses.
Thanks for welcoming me into the family
(even though we all know how that *turned out).*
Much love to you, dearies,
every season of the year.
XOX

Contents

One

Perfect submission, all is at rest,
I in my Savior am happy and blest;
Watching and waiting, looking above,
Filled with His goodness, **lost in His love.**

—FANNY CROSBY, "BLESSED ASSURANCE," 1873

A Season of Grace

*S*he sat in the pew across from us, dressed entirely in yellow. No more than four years old, she was utterly adorable, from the circlet of yellow flowers in her hair to her lacy dress, pale tights, and Mary Jane shoes.

But here's what struck me. This little girl hadn't simply come to church. *She'd come to see God.*

When we stood to sing "He lives! He lives!" she jumped up on the cushioned pew and kept on jumping, clapping her hands in perfect rhythm with the pipe organ. With each verse she grew more animated, not seeking attention, but simply caught up in the joy of the moment. While the rest of us sang, she worshiped.

What if I did that? I wondered. *What if I offered God my whole self, nothing held back?*

Despite her grandmother's patient attempts to put a lid on all that enthusiasm, the girl just couldn't help it. When the last chord rang out, her upturned face shone like the sun as she stretched up her hands to celebrate Jesus.

I don't know her name, but I hope it's *Mary.* She has all the makings of a woman of Easter: joyful, hopeful, faithful.

In the pages to come, we'll meet three women of Easter who poured out their lives for their beloved Teacher in much the same way the women of Christmas—Elizabeth, Mary, and Anna—honored and served the infant Jesus. Mary of Bethany prepared the Lord for burial by anointing Him with a priceless perfume. Mary of Nazareth, who'd watched Jesus draw His first breath, bravely watched Him breathe His last. Mary Magdalene witnessed His resurrection and proclaimed the good news to His disciples.

Amazing. Amazing. Amazing.

When you turn the page, you'll find our journey begins on a somber note. Jesus is our greatest source of joy, but He is also "a man of sorrows, and acquainted with grief."[1] All through Advent we anticipate His birth. All through Lent we anticipate His death.

The word *Lent* means "the lengthening of daylight hours," the coming of spring, when purple and white crocuses push through the hard ground, promising warmer days to come. In many churches the forty weekdays from Ash Wednesday to Easter are devoted to fasting and abstinence, honoring the Lord's forty days in the wilderness.[2] Some believers focus on repentance and prayer during the Lenten season. Others scrub their houses even as they ask the Lord to cleanse them of bad thoughts and bad habits. Many of us choose to give up something for Lent, fully aware that nothing can compare to the life Jesus laid down for us.

His sacrifice is the heart of the story. But not the end of the story.

The Lord's resurrection is the most glorious, victorious moment in history. You and I will watch these ancient scenes unfold through the eyes of three women who were witnesses, who were there. Just the thought gives me goose bumps.

All three Marys will show us what happens when we encounter the love of our Savior and are transformed. That's what Lent is all about. A time of renewal. A season of grace.

I'm *so* glad you're here.

Lost in His Love

*H*e was dying. Of that Mary of Bethany was certain. She knelt beside him, fresh tears spilling down her cheeks. Her beloved brother, Lazarus, lay on a narrow bed, his skin as dull and lifeless as his dun-colored tunic. A twisted cord hung loosely around his waist. His chest looked sunken, empty.

Mary wept in silence, smoothing her hand over his brow, longing for answers. *We need You, Jesus.* He alone could heal her brother, make him well again, make him whole. If she sent word, would He come? *Please, Lord.*

> Now a man named Lazarus was sick. He was from
> Bethany, the village of Mary and her sister Martha.
> *John 11:1*

The original Greek tells us Lazarus was "weak, feeble."[1] He was not suffering from a common cold or an abscessed tooth. No, this illness held little promise of recovery. If you've lost a sibling, if you've walked in Mary's footsteps, then you understand her sorrow.

Sadly, I know Mary's heartache all too well.

When the first e-mail about my brother Tom appeared in my inbox, I assumed his liver disease was curable. Surgery. Medicine. There had to be a solution. He was fifteen years older than I was, but he wasn't old.

This was the brother who took me canoeing, who showed me the beauty of nature, who talked our mother into letting me keep the kitten I brought home from the PTA festival. Tom was caring, funny, and wise, and he loved the little sister he called Rootie Toot.

As e-mails turned into lengthy phone calls, the reports grew dire. "Months." "Weeks." My sisters and I planned a trip west to see him, hoping Tom would rally and prove the doctors wrong. We loved him desperately. But we could not save him and arrived too late to say good-bye. Even now, years later, the missed opportunity and the tragic loss still weigh heavily on our hearts. It's an ache that never goes away, a missing piece that can't be replaced.

Mary of Bethany and her sister, Martha, surely felt the same way about their brother, Lazarus. Helpless, almost hopeless. Longing for their good friend Jesus to rescue him. It's been rightly said "the sickness of those we love is our affliction."[2] Mary and Martha shared their brother's every wince of pain, every halting breath.

Before we continue with their story, let's step back to the first biblical scene that features these women encountering Jesus. We'll do this not only to understand them better but also to learn more about the One these sisters loved and served.

> As Jesus and his disciples were on their way, he came to a village where a woman named Martha opened her home to him. *Luke 10:38*

The village, situated in a pleasant spot surrounded by fine trees,[3] is not named here, but the woman is. "A certain woman" (ASV) called Martha. Since the passage mentions "her home," Martha was likely the oldest sibling and therefore head of the household, the one in charge.[4]

Picture a two-story house built of limestone with a dirt floor and a broad outer stairway leading to an upper room.[5] An enclosed courtyard, meant for socializing and cooking, was shared by Martha and her neighbors.[6]

Since we find no mention in the Bible of parents, spouses, or children for Martha and her siblings and no gainful employment is described, they may have received a sizable inheritance.[7] If so, we'll soon see it was well spent to care for those in need.

Like a first-century Martha Stewart, Martha of Bethany threw open her door to this itinerant preacher, this miracle worker capable of casting out demons and healing the sick. She may not have grasped the whole of it yet, that He was "God manifest in the flesh."[8] But Martha knew what was required—food and shelter—and that was enough for her.

Now a confession: I'm not a confident hostess. If a friend stops by unannounced, I've been known to stand on our back porch and talk to her rather than invite her to come in and sit at my kitchen table. Why? Because it has crumbs on it. Because the sink is full of dishes. Because I might be expected to serve her something worth eating. Because I'm still learning how to "offer hospitality to one another"[9] without fear of disappointing people.

Yet Martha gladly opened her home. Impressive.

> She had a sister called Mary, who sat at the Lord's feet
> listening to what he said. *Luke 10:39*

Though Martha was head of the house, "Mary seems to have been its heart."[10] We picture her seated on the floor—quiet, attentive, devoted. Not goofing off, not daydreaming, not avoiding work. Just listening instead of speaking. "We *hear* Martha; we *see* Mary."[11]

Having "settled down at the Lord's feet" (PHILLIPS), Mary of Bethany fixed her gaze on Jesus. From her vantage point, no one else was in the room. What was Mary listening to? Literally, "the word of him." In Greek, the *logos* of Him.[12] "In the beginning was the Word, and the Word was with God, and the Word was God."[13] She wasn't merely hearing His voice. She was "hearing the word" (YLT).

No wonder she didn't move.

In the first century, sitting at a teacher's feet was the mark of a disciple, a follower, a faithful student. The apostle Paul explained, "At the feet of Gamaliel I was educated."[14] It was a physical position meant to show humility, respect, and a willingness to listen. Jesus, who invited His followers to "learn from me,"[15] welcomed Mary of Bethany in His traveling classroom in an era when Jewish females were relegated to the women's section in the back of a synagogue, hidden behind a screen.[16]

I stood in a similar place one October morning in Prague, visiting the oldest active synagogue in Europe, built in the thirteenth century.[17] On the western side was a dim outer corridor with small openings high up on the wall, permitting women to listen to the Torah being read inside the synagogue proper. Imagine our medieval sisters huddled beside those rough stones, straining to hear. Yet centuries earlier Mary of Bethany listened and learned at her Savior's feet right beside his male disciples.

Jesus did not rebuke Mary or remind her of her place. He made room for her. He invited her to stay. Gently but firmly Jesus defied the culture and set people free, finding "no need to enforce the strictest gender-role customs of his time."[18] If Mary wanted to sit at His feet, she was most welcome.

> But Martha was distracted by all the preparations that had to be made. *Luke 10:40*

I always pay attention to the *but*s of the Bible. A few letters, easily overlooked, the word *but* raises a red flag each time it shows up. Here *but* makes a comparison—"by contrast" (CEB) Martha was distracted.

Distracted. We know what that looks like. Martha didn't need the Internet or a smart phone to divert her attention. The Greek word for "distracted" comes from a verb meaning "to draw away,"[19] like dragging a heavy sword out of its scabbard. Martha was "pulled away by all she had to do" (MSG) and became "overly occupied and too busy" (AMPC) to pay attention to their honored guest.

True, her preparations were her means of service, her brand of ministry. Martha was doing good things. Godly things. Useful things.

But . . .

> She came to him and asked, . . . *Luke 10:40*

This wasn't as polite as it sounds. Martha "burst in" (PHILLIPS), "interrupting them" (MSG). Mary remained seated while Martha stood before Jesus, in His face, determined to be seen and heard.

> . . . "Lord, don't you care that my sister has left me to
> do the work by myself?" *Luke 10:40*

Really, Martha? *No one* cares like Jesus. Even so, she was convinced He would agree with her. "Doesn't it seem unfair?" (NLT), she asked Him. Or here's the LRV, the Lizzie Revised Version: "I'm upset. Aren't you upset?" The original Greek suggests Martha felt "left behind, neglected, forsaken"[20] by her younger sister, who was "completely oblivious to all the fussing and fuming of her sister— even Martha's disapproving looks did not penetrate."[21]

Any hostess who has slaved away in the kitchen while her family and guests enjoyed themselves in the living room can empathize with Martha. In her day a woman's tasks included grinding flour, baking bread, tending the garden, spinning wool, washing clothes, and cooking all the food.[22] I can push the Start button on my microwave oven and throw in a load of laundry, but that long list of tasks? Whoa. Easy to see why Martha was weary.

> "Tell her to help me!" *Luke 10:40*

The exclamation point reveals all we need to know about her mood at the moment. We can see and hear this "harried, frustrated woman . . . bossing around the Creator of the universe."[23] Rather than confront her sister directly, Martha asked Jesus to intervene. "Tell her to get up and help me!" (PHILLIPS).

Now it was Martha's turn to learn from the Teacher.

I wonder if Jesus shook His head when He said her name. Twice.

"Martha, Martha," the Lord answered, "you are worried and upset about many things, . . ." *Luke 10:41*

"Martha, Martha." The repetition was a "tender rebuke."[24] Rather than applaud her work ethic, the Lord chided her for "fretting" (CJB) and "fussing" (MSG). "His concern was not for the state of her home and table, but for the state of her soul and her heart."[25]

No question about it, Jesus was scolding Martha. Not because what she did was unimportant or unnecessary, but because Martha thought her efforts were of greater significance than Mary's.

We know this woman. We *are* this woman. We fret, fuss, and find a dozen reasons to be unhappy when we feel overworked or underappreciated. Perhaps that's why the Bible introduces us to these two sisters side by side—to show us by example what God values most.

Jesus, who once cautioned His followers, "Do not work for food that spoils, but for food that endures to eternal life,"[26] was urging Martha to change her focus from standing in the kitchen to kneeling at His feet.

". . . but few things are needed—or indeed only one." *Luke 10:42*

The things we actually *need* would make a short list. Very short. For those who believe in the name of Jesus, there's "only one thing that is essential" (CJB). Rather than fancy meals or tidy rooms, what matters most is Jesus Himself. "Martha thought Christ had need of her and of her services, but Mary knew that it was she that needed Christ."[27]

The truth? Martha's well-tended house long ago turned to dust. Every wooden lintel, every clay lamp, every leather sandal gone. But Jesus? He is with us still and will be forever. Mary of Bethany grasped that truth and chose wisely.

"Mary has chosen what is better, . . ." *Luke 10:42*

"Martha had chosen duty and Mary had chosen Jesus."[28] Mary knew the difference between temporal and eternal. "Her soul had one great want,"[29] and it wasn't matching wine cups. She wanted Jesus. His presence, His teaching, His brotherly affection—these satisfied her deepest longings.

We know the one thing for Mary. And Jesus assures us that a relationship with Him is ours to keep.

". . . and it will not be taken away from her." *Luke 10:42*

Physical things can be snatched from our hands but not His mercy, His grace, His wisdom. They are sealed within us by the Holy Spirit.

As a devout Jew, Mary surely knew the psalms. We can imagine her whispering in her heart—or aloud so He might hear— "LORD, you alone are my portion and my cup; you make my lot secure."[30]

Mary understood what mattered most. If we learn from her, "if we become women who seek the one 'needful' thing, we will see our lives transformed."[31] Such transformation isn't a selfish longing. It's what Christ wants most for us: "To be made new in the attitude of your minds; and to put on the new self, created to be like God in true righteousness and holiness."[32]

Mary of Bethany had that aim from the start, it seemed. Martha was learning from her example and, most of all, from the Master Teacher. Though Jesus knew their temperaments were poles apart, it's clear that He loved and understood both of them and thought no less of one than the other.[33] He didn't favor one kind of personality, didn't suggest that women could serve Him in only one way. In the kingdom of God "there is need for both vigorous caregiving and quiet listening."[34] These women exemplified both possibilities.

Now that we've met the sisters, let's return to our opening scene with their ailing brother, Lazarus. He, too, needed a Savior.

> So the sisters sent word to Jesus, "Lord, the one you love is sick." *John 11:3*

When they dispatched a messenger to search for the Master, they didn't say "Come running," but surely that's what the sisters prayed He would do.

Lazarus is described as the one Jesus loved. The Greek word here, *philos,* means "beloved, dear, friendly."[35] This is the kind of love siblings share, which goes far deeper than a casual friendship. Mary and Martha reminded Jesus how much He cared for Lazarus, perhaps to ensure His swift response. After all, their brother's Hebrew name meant "God has helped."[36] A reason to hope, then. A reason to ask.

They "sent someone to tell Jesus" (ERV) that Lazarus was sick but not that he was dying. In that time and place, with little more than medicinal herbs on hand, any ailment could quickly lead to a tragic end. This family needed more than a pastoral visit. They needed the Great Physician.

Meanwhile, Jesus was in the countryside across the Jordan River in Bethabara, where John the Baptist began his ministry.[37] Bethabara, perhaps twenty miles east of Bethany, was a single day's journey on foot. The messenger found Jesus there and conveyed the sad news about Lazarus and his illness.

> When he heard this, Jesus said, "This sickness will not end in death." *John 11:4*

Only a God who knows the future could offer such hope! Though "the man is sick" (WE), Jesus told those around Him, "this illness isn't fatal" (CEB). With His own death and resurrection on the horizon, Jesus wanted them to know that Lazarus's story would end well. And so would His.

Jesus was assuring His people that God the Father would be with them through the painful days to come—the waiting, the sorrow, the grief. Even if "God does not spare those he loves from life's difficulties,"[38] He does promise to bring us through and make the journey worthwhile.

> "No, it is for God's glory so that God's Son may be glorified through it." *John 11:4*

It's deeply comforting to know that sickness, even death, is purposeful. Not random, not meaningless, not "Oh, what a shame." Everything that happened to Lazarus was designed to "bring glory to God and his Son" (CEV). A wonderful plan, though extremely difficult for Lazarus and his sisters, who couldn't fathom the joy that was to come, who didn't know that "our light and momentary troubles are achieving for us an eternal glory that far outweighs them all."[39]

What they clung to—and what we must cling to as well—is the Lord's immeasurable and unconditional love. He knows our needs and He meets them. He sees our hurts and He heals them. He understands our fears and He overcomes them.

> Now Jesus loved Martha and her sister and Lazarus.
> *John 11:5*

So personal and so endearing. An entire verse to capture the Lord's deep affection for three ordinary people. The Greek tells us His love for them was "ongoing, continuing."[40] Not a one-time thing but an all-the-time thing. These siblings from Bethany "were His dear friends, and He held them in loving esteem" (AMPC).

Interesting that Martha and Lazarus are mentioned by name but Mary is not. We find only the Greek word for "sister,"[41] yet each person is listed separately and emphatically with the word *and* between them. Jesus loved Martha *and* her sister *and* Lazarus, personally and individually. As we say in the online world, these were His friends In Real Life.

The Greek word for "loved" in this passage is *agapaó*.[42] It's a higher, more spiritual form of love and conveys a sense of preference, of being chosen. Jesus not only loved these followers, but He also made an eternal investment in His relationship with them, just as He has with us.

His friendship is "deeper, closer, and more tender still, in which all believers have their share."[43] Mary and Martha embraced

His love like the lifeline it is. Have you done the same, friend? Do you know how much He loves you and how precious you are to Him?

Though Jesus responded to the news of Lazarus's illness in a way that might seem unfeeling, even cruel, don't lose heart. This is Jesus we're talking about.

> So when he heard that Lazarus was sick, he stayed where he was two more days, . . . *John 11:6*

Hmm. Knowing His close friend was sick, shouldn't Jesus at least have gone to see him? To comfort Lazarus? To pray for him? Instead—and rather "oddly" (msg)—Jesus "stayed where he was" (ceb). Two. Long. Days. He got the news but didn't move.

Here's why: He loved them and planned to do "something great and extraordinary for them."[44] It would be a miracle unlike any other He'd performed. People had witnessed Him heal wounds, cure diseases, cast out demons, banish blindness, even resuscitate someone newly deceased. What He planned for Lazarus required more time. Christ's followers needed to see that resurrection was possible even several days after a body was buried in a tomb.

While Jesus tarried by the Jordan, two women in Bethany watched their brother slip away from them. His final hours are not described in God's Word, but we can imagine what they were like. Agonizing for Lazarus. Devastating for his sisters.

In our darkest moments, when we cry out to God and wonder if He's listening, He sometimes whispers, *Wait.* It's a hard word to hear yet comforting as well. It means He is there, He is with us, and He has a plan, even if it is not our plan.

Then Lazarus's heart stopped beating. The brother they loved was gone.

So hard, my sisters. So hard.

All hope abandoned, Mary and Martha prepared their brother's body, anointing him with myrrh and wrapping him in graveclothes. According to Jewish custom, a corpse was to be laid in a burial cave as quickly as possible.[45] The sisters could not delay. Besides, if Jesus *did* walk through their door, it would be too late.

But with the Lord it's never too late.

Mind if I say that again? *With Jesus it's never too late.* Never too late for Him to mend a relationship you thought was broken. Never too late for Him to help you get clean, get sober, get a new start. Never too late for Him to work a miracle in your life.

He's on His way, beloved.

> . . . and then he said to his disciples, "Let us go back to Judea." *John 11:7*

"We should go" (ERV), He told his men in Bethabara. It wasn't a suggestion. The Greek means "to lead."[46] The Lord was fully aware of what had happened in Bethany and knew it was time to return.

See how carefully He chose His words.

> . . . he went on to tell them, "Our friend Lazarus has fallen asleep; but I am going there to wake him up." *John 11:11*

The disciples missed the Lord's veiled reference to death. They thought only of the literal meaning—"to awaken out of sleep"[47]—and told Jesus that if Lazarus remained in bed, he would surely get better. These men were clueless about the miracle required to stir Lazarus. When Jesus said, "I go to raise him from sleep" (wyc), the key word was *raise*.

It seemed Jesus needed to explain further. They had to understand.

> So then he told them plainly, "Lazarus is dead, . . ."
> *John 11:14*

Their eyes must have widened in disbelief. *Dead?* The word sounded so cold, so final. Yet Jesus spoke about His friend's demise "openly" (wyc) and "freely" (ylt). From the Lord's standpoint, Lazarus was merely sleeping—a minor issue for One who would conquer the grave. As Paul later wrote to the believers at Thessalonica, "Brothers and sisters, we do not want you to be uninformed about those who sleep in death, so that you do not grieve like the rest of mankind, who have no hope."[48]

Hope was exactly what Jesus offered His disciples that day on the banks of the Jordan, wanting to strengthen their faith and prepare them for the challenging days ahead. As we read these words, their hope becomes our hope. Death is not the end for those who love the Lord. It's the beginning of a new and forever life.

> ". . . and for your sake I am glad I was not there, so that you may believe." *John 11:15*

Jesus stated clearly His intended purpose: He wanted His disciples "to trust and rely" (ampc) on Him. "Now you will have a chance to put your faith in me" (CEV), He told them. "Now you will really believe" (NLT).

Weren't they already believers? Yes, in the same way many of us are. We identify ourselves as Christian, we attend church, we put money in the offering plate, and we pray. Jesus was asking His disciples to take another step—if not a leap—and trust Him completely in every situation, however difficult or uncertain.

Though we may believe with our heads, Jesus wants us to believe with our whole hearts. To place our lives in His hands and put our faith in God, who is "trustworthy in all he promises and faithful in all he does."[49]

Mary of Bethany believed in Him. Martha did too. Even so, Jesus said to His followers, "You're about to be given new grounds for believing" (MSG).

That's what we want, Lord, this Easter and always. We want to believe.

Believe in His power to change us. Believe He can bring us back to life.

Two

Martha then her sister called;
Mary went to meet the Lord.
When she reached Him, knelt in tears,
Seeking comfort from His word.

—Susan H. Peterson, "One Named Lazarus," 2000

Mary Went to
Meet the Lord

*azarus was gone.*

Mary of Bethany could think of nothing else. Her brother had died in her arms, gasping for breath. Perhaps if Jesus had come in time . . .

But He hadn't come at all. Three days had passed. The messenger had returned but not Jesus.

I thought You loved my brother, Lord. I thought You loved us all.

Shrouded in grief, Mary could not comprehend why the Lord was delayed. Yet imagine how long those days of waiting must have been for Jesus! Knowing Lazarus had died. Knowing the sisters had lost hope.

The sooner He returned to Bethany, the better.

"But let us go to him." *John 11:15*

We sense the urgency in the Lord's voice as He again told the disciples with Him in Bethabara, "Let's go to him now" (EXB). The Lord knew what He would find—a dead body wrapped in linen and placed in a tomb like the one where His own body would soon rest. Undaunted by death's grip on His friend, Jesus hastened to Bethany to see Mary and Martha.

The quiet village of Bethany stood on the southeastern slope of the Mount of Olives,[1] no more than four miles from the little town of Bethlehem, where Jesus was born. He knew the area well and didn't waste another moment getting there.

> On his arrival, Jesus found that Lazarus had already been in the tomb for four days. *John 11:17*

Why four days? Because it all adds up. One day for the messenger to reach Him, two days for Him to tarry, plus another day's journey back to Bethany. But it's more than simple math. "Some Jews believed that a soul would stay near a body for up to three days after death."[2] A fourth day in the grave guaranteed a body was truly dead and its soul departed.

> Now Bethany was less than two miles from Jerusalem, . . . *John 11:18*

Here's why the short distance is mentioned: Bethany was an easy walk from Jerusalem. Even before Jesus arrived, the sisters had company and were not alone in their grieving.

> . . . and many Jews had come to Martha and Mary to comfort them in the loss of their brother. *John 11:19*

The scene isn't fully described for us, but we can imagine the two sisters "swallowed up with sorrow,"[3] seated on the floor, weeping, while other women mourned and wailed. Friends bent down to offer comfort. The Greek word for "comfort" means "to speak by the side of."[4] The name of the deceased was whispered in reverent tones, each visitor in turn lamenting the man's passing.

In the Jewish culture there's "a strong belief that when a righteous man dies, the world suffers loss. The balance of righteousness versus evil tips in the wrong direction."[5] Who wouldn't mourn the loss of a good man like Lazarus?

Then news came. A neighbor perhaps, running ahead of the Lord and His disciples, breathlessly announced His approach.

> When Martha heard that Jesus was coming, she went out to meet him, . . . *John 11:20*

Big sister was on the move. Rather than wait inside the house for Jesus to arrive, Martha—a "bustling, impetuous person whose major interest was action"[6]—leaped to her feet and "went out to greet him" (ERV).

What about her younger sister, Mary? Didn't she run to welcome Him too?

She did not.

> . . . but Mary stayed at home. *John 11:20*

Mary didn't simply *stay* at home. She *sat down* at home, as the original Greek makes clear.[7] While her sister took off, Mary remained "still" (KJV). Not because she was exhausted from crying or weary with grief. Mary "was sitting shivah" (OJB), the Hebrew word for "seven."[8] As Jewish custom dictated, immediately after the burial of a close relative, family members gathered in the home of the deceased, with their outer garments ritually torn, and received visitors for seven full days.[9]

While Mary "kept sitting" (YLT), Martha, true to form, kept talking.

> "Lord," Martha said to Jesus, "if you had been here,
> my brother would not have died." *John 11:21*

Wait. Was she scolding Jesus? Was she saying this never would have happened if He'd returned sooner? "I wish you had been here!" (NIrV). We've seen bold Martha in action before, quick to speak her mind. Was she mad? Disappointed? Frustrated? Confused?

Her next words give us the answer: none of the above.

> "But I know that even now God will give you whatever
> you ask." *John 11:22*

Ah. Instead of being fueled with anger, Martha was filled with "a loving faith in Jesus' power to heal."[10] When she said, "God will," that was trust talking, not doubt or fear. "Whatever you ask from God, God will grant you" (NET), Martha declared. "I still believe" (VOICE).

Bless her spunky, faithful self.

In response Jesus assured her that Lazarus was not gone forever.

> Jesus said to her, "Your brother will rise again." *John
> 11:23*

Sounds like the kind of thing we say to one another at funerals. "He's in a better place" or "You'll see her again someday." That's apparently what Martha thought Jesus meant.

> Martha answered, "I know he will rise again in the resurrection at the last day." *John 11:24*

She didn't say, "I think." She said, "I know." However great her heartache, Martha was certain she would see her brother at the end of days.

Then Jesus pushed her faith to the next level.

> Jesus said to her, "I am the resurrection and the life." *John 11:25*

He wanted to make this truth abundantly clear for Martha's sake and for ours. *"Resurrection is not something I do—I AM the resurrection."*[11] No one but Jesus can conquer the grave. Resurrection power is His alone. "I am the one who raises the dead to life!" (CEV). Perhaps for the first time Martha fully understood that "God himself was standing before her, speaking to her, loving her."[12]

Then He made a mind-boggling, eternity-spanning promise.

> "The one who believes in me will live, even though they die; . . ." *John 11:25*

Imagine it! Anyone who "adheres to, trusts in, and relies on" (AMPC) Jesus will also overcome the grave. Put aside any concerns about "Will I get into heaven?" If you believe in Him, friend, you will live forever. "By his power God raised the Lord from the dead, and he will raise us also."[13]

Jesus had another promise for Martha, more astounding than the first.

> ". . . and whoever lives by believing in me will never die." *John 11:26*

But won't our bodies eventually wear out? Won't the usual procession of flowers and sympathy cards and memorial services follow in the wake of our passing? Yes, but our *souls* will live on. "The body's death to this world is the soul's birth into another world."[14] The soul is the eternal part of us. "The end result of your faith [is] the salvation of your souls."[15] Jesus didn't lay down His life to save our bodies. He died and rose again to save our souls.

Then Jesus asked Martha the Big Question, the one we all must answer.

> "Do you believe this?" *John 11:26*

This means all of it: who He is and why He came and what that means for us.

Martha didn't hesitate, didn't tell Him "I'll get back to you." Her response was swift and sure, "a staggering expression of faith."[16]

> "Yes, Lord," she replied, "I believe that you are the Messiah, the Son of God, who is to come into the world." *John 11:27*

Go, Martha! When Jesus said, "I am," she affirmed, "You are." Her "I believe" confession is remarkable because she stated His title, His divine nature, and His calling. Neither Peter nor John made this bold proclamation that day in Bethany. A *woman* did. God's woman. Martha's faith was now as solid and unshakable as her sister's. She who served the food also dished out the truth: "It is for Your coming that the world has waited" (AMPC).

What Martha did you and I can do as well. Profess our faith. Proclaim His truth. Promote His kingdom. This isn't a one-hour-a-week Jesus we're dealing with. Someone we sing praises to on Sunday morning and forget about on Sunday afternoon. He expects and deserves nothing less than our total commitment.

For us every day can be Easter. Every day can be a celebration. "He is risen!"

> After she had said this, she went back and called her sister Mary aside. *John 11:28*

What a spiritual turning point for Martha! Having made her bold statement of faith, she "ran home to Mary" (VOICE) and beckoned her to move away from the mourners so Martha could speak to her "privately" (CEB). The Greek word means "secretly,"[17] adding a layer of intrigue. Maybe Martha didn't want everyone rushing out to meet Jesus until Mary had His undivided attention. If so, it was a generous move on Martha's part. "There was a time when Martha would have called Mary away from Jesus; now she calls her sister to him."[18]

Shared grief had undoubtedly glued these two women together. When we attended my brother's memorial service, my sisters and I shared a hotel room, sat side by side at the service, and linked arms often. In times of loss, faith and family matter most.

Then Martha whispered the news in Mary's ear.

> "The Teacher is here," she said, "and is asking for you."
> *John 11:28*

Mary's pulse surely quickened, knowing the One who loved them was "close at hand" (AMPC) and wanted to speak with her.

We can only guess the questions that darted through Mary's mind. Would Jesus apologize for His delayed return? Offer His condolences? Ask how He might still be helpful? Martha provided no details, only that Jesus was "calling" (CJB) for Mary. The Greek word for "call" is a familiar one—*phóneó*,[19] the source of our modern word *phone.*

And this call needed to be answered.

> When Mary heard this, she got up quickly and went to him. *John 11:29*

All that Mary of Bethany needed to know was that Jesus wanted to see her, and she headed out the door. Never mind what the other mourners might think of her abandoning her post. She didn't seek their advice, ask their leave, or beg their pardon. Fact is, "Mary did not waste a minute" (VOICE).

She "jumped" (CJB). She "sprang" (AMPC). She "rose" (RSV). The same Greek word is used to describe Jesus's resurrection. Even before He raised her brother from the dead, Jesus raised Mary from her mourning.

> Now Jesus had not yet entered the village, but was still
> at the place where Martha had met him. *John 11:30*

He waited for Mary on the outskirts of Bethany, having "not yet come into the town" (KJV). We can picture Jesus standing among the olive trees on a hilly rise not far from Jerusalem. Watching for Mary. Determined to bring an end to her suffering.

> When the Jews who had been with Mary in the house,
> comforting her, noticed how quickly she got up and
> went out, . . . *John 11:31*

The unnamed mourners, "her sympathizing Jewish friends" (MSG), move to the foreground of our story. One minute Mary was sitting, and the next "they saw her stand and leave quickly" (EXB). *What's up with that?* they surely wondered. She didn't tell them where she was going or invite them to go with her.

But they went anyway.

> . . . they followed her, supposing she was going to the
> tomb to mourn there. *John 11:31*

Interesting. They didn't follow Martha on her mad dash out the door, but they did trail after Mary, "thinking she was on her way to the tomb to weep" (MSG). Apparently the one reason Mary could gracefully leave her post was to go "to Lazarus's grave" (NLT) and "pour out her grief" (AMPC).

Though they followed Mary of Bethany that day, the mourners weren't all followers of Christ. Not yet.

> When Mary reached the place where Jesus was and saw
> him, she fell at his feet . . . *John 11:32*

A common posture for Mary. "As soon as she saw him" (CEV), she "dropped down" (AMPC) to the ground. When we first met her, she was seated at His feet, listening to Him. Here she fell at His feet, "overwhelmed with a passionate sorrow."[20] Her physical position reveals her humble attitude and helps us imagine how she might have sounded when she spoke these words, her voice breaking and her heart as well:

> . . . "Lord, if you had been here, my brother would not
> have died." *John 11:32*

Sound familiar? It's the very thing Martha had said moments earlier—a word-for-word match in the original Greek. Maybe the sisters had often repeated this phrase during the last four days so that these were the first words on their lips when they saw Him. "Master, if only you had been here" (MSG).

What Mary *didn't* say is telling. Unlike Martha—her believing, proclaiming sister—Mary didn't state that God would give His Son whatever He asked for.

Is it possible (oh dear) that Mary was expressing a lack of faith and revealing the depth of her disappointment that Christ hadn't come sooner? Or was she merely asking an honest question: "Where were You, Lord?" Maybe she meant only to acknowledge His power and surrender to it, realizing "He was the Solution. To everything. To anything."[21]

All we can be certain of are the two truths she shared: "I wish you had been here!" (NIrV) and "my brother would not have died!"

(GNT). They are the only words spoken by Mary of Bethany that are recorded in Scripture, and they are fraught with emotion and perhaps a faint thread of guilt.

When a loved one passes away, "if onlys" often haunt our thoughts for weeks, months, even years after the funeral.

"If only I'd called that morning . . ."

"If only I'd insisted on a second opinion . . ."

"If only I'd stopped by on my way to work . . ."

"If only I'd helped him stay on his meds . . ."

"If only I'd made more time for her . . ."

Don't go there, beloved. God knows the hour of each person's passing. Whatever we did or didn't do for someone we loved, the timing of his or her departure was God's alone. "Thy will be done"[22] is more than a prayer request. It's a foregone conclusion.

Mary surely knew this truth. Yet "when she ran to Him, she didn't begin a theological discussion. Instead, she fell at His feet,"[23] unable to hold back her tears.

> When Jesus saw her weeping, and the Jews who
> had come along with her also weeping, . . . *John
> 11:33*

He could hardly ignore her "profound grief" (VOICE) or the "moaning and weeping of her companions" (VOICE). We can almost hear them "crying" (CEV) and "sobbing" (MSG), their misery unabated.

If we see a stranger in tears, we might feel a sympathetic sting in our eyes. But when a person we care about is crying, then we "weep with those who weep"[24] because we know them. And because we love them.

Jesus loved Mary of Bethany. Naturally He was affected by her tears.

> . . . he was deeply moved in spirit and troubled. *John 11:33*

There's more going on here than meets the eye. Jesus "groaned" (ASV), "sighed" (AMPC), and was "visibly distressed" (PHILLIPS)—not from angst as much as anger. This passage "ought to be rendered, 'He breathed indignation.'"[25] Jesus was mad? Yes, He was. The Word tells us He became "enraged in the Spirit" (JUB) and "a deep anger welled up within him" (NLT).

In truth, Jesus was so "disturbed" (CEB) that He "made noise" (WYC). The Greek word for "troubled" means "to snort with anger,"[26] like a horse showing its displeasure. Try it. Yes, that sound, followed by these words:

> "Where have you laid him?" he asked. *John 11:34*

Was He frustrated with her tears? Disgusted at her lack of faith? Not our compassionate Savior. Rather, He was angry with death itself and the grave's power to rob His people of joy, of fellowship, of hope. When He asked, "Where have you put his body?" (CEV), Jesus was ready to put an end to their suffering.

Perhaps these words from the prophet Hosea beat in the Lord's heart as He strode toward Lazarus's grave:

> "I will deliver this people from the power of
> the grave;
> I will redeem them from death.

Where, O death, are your plagues?

Where, O grave, is your destruction?" *Hosea 13:14*

Lazarus lay in a nearby tomb. But where exactly? Jesus could have prayed and asked His Father to lead Him. Instead, He asked Mary of Bethany and the others to show Him the way so they would be present when the miracle unfolded.

"Come and see, Lord," they replied. *John 11:34*

The Greek word for "see" means more than simply "look upon."[27] It's an invitation to serve as a witness and to perceive what's going on. Just as we might say to a friend, "Will you look at that?"

What happened next was tender, sacred, and unexpected. Captured in a verse with only two words—famous for its brevity but far more for its depth of emotion—this may be the "strongest expression of Jesus' existence as a human being."[28]

Jesus wept. *John 11:35*

He did, dear sister. The Son of God wept. A great sadness swept over Him, moving Him to tears. We cannot know what He was thinking and feeling at the moment, but we can be sure of this: He felt their sorrow in a deeply personal way, just as He feels ours. When we suffer, He suffers with us. When we grieve, He grieves.

The night my brother passed away, the terrible news came in a text message. Please understand: we have a huge family. Calling everyone individually would have taken hours. A message on our phones allowed all of us to find out at the same time and as quickly as possible.

I was sitting on a hotel bed when the text arrived. Though I'd steeled myself for bad news, I still wasn't prepared. My hands shook as I read the words "Lizzie, dear, your brother left this world at 6:27 p.m. Mountain Time . . ." There was more, but I couldn't bear to read it. A great sob poured out as I threw the phone across the bed. Not in anger but in despair. *It can't be true. It can't be.*

Every emotion flooded through me as I wept, pressing a washcloth to my face, trying to stem the flow. The thought of never seeing Tom again was more than I could bear. I wept until I could weep no more, and then I wept again.

Perhaps that's how Jesus cried that day. Not just one tear running down His cheek but a steady stream flowing from the depths of His heart. People took notice and were moved.

> Then the Jews said, "See how he loved him!" *John 11:36*

"Behold" (DRA), the Jewish mourners cried out. "He loved Lazarus very much!" (ERV). Yes, He did. And loved him still.

Our love for people doesn't end when they pass away. More often our feelings deepen as we realize how much they mean to us and how dearly we miss them. Though my mother died when I was twenty-three, I love her now more than ever. My affection for her grew deeper once I became a mother. Deeper still when I reached the age my mother was when she gave birth to me. Even deeper when I lost my father.

Love transcends the grave, as Mary of Bethany and her sister were about to discover.

> Jesus, once more deeply moved, came to the tomb. It
> was a cave with a stone laid across the entrance. *John
> 11:38*

Still upset and "groaning in himself" (DRA), Jesus walked the short distance to the grave, which was little more than "a simple cave in the hillside" (MSG). As was the custom, "a boulder was lying against it" (AMP).

How familiar all this sounds. A tomb. A stone. A body about to be resurrected. A startling display of divine love and immense power. A rehearsal of Easter morning.

> "Take away the stone," he said. *John 11:39*

Despite the clarity of His command, no one moved. Only Martha was brave enough to speak up.

> "But, Lord," said Martha, the sister of the dead man,
> "by this time there is a bad odor, for he has been there
> four days." *John 11:39*

Always the practical one, Martha was concerned about the "offensive odor" (AMP) that would fill the air—something no hostess wants for her guests. She reminded the Lord, "He has been dead four days!" (AMPC). As if Jesus did not already know that. As if the "bad smell" (CEV) mattered or the number of days had any bearing on a miracle.

> Then Jesus said, "Did I not tell you that if you believe,
> you will see the glory of God?" *John 11:40*

Oh yes, we remember His pointed question a few minutes earlier—"Do you believe this?"[29]—and Martha's swift affirmation. But no response is recorded here in Scripture. Not from Martha or Mary of Bethany or the disciples who traveled with Jesus or the Jews who followed Mary to the tomb.

We're not even told who moved the stone. But someone did.

> So they took away the stone. *John 11:41*

Yes, we can see the men quickly backing up, fearful of the stench and even more afraid of what might happen next. While the crowd murmured, Mary and Martha clung to each other, staring at the open tomb.

> Then Jesus looked up and said, "Father, I thank you that you have heard me." *John 11:41*

He "looked up." Not to see His Father or to be seen by Him, but to show those around Him where their hope and their help came from. Often we turn to one another for answers. Jesus shows us a better way. *Look up.* "What is prayer, but the ascent of the soul to God?"[30]

> "I knew that you always hear me, but I said this for the benefit of the people standing here, that they may believe that you sent me." *John 11:42*

Imagine the Son of God having an open conversation with His heavenly Father! Any onlookers who doubted were about to be fully convinced.

When he had said this, Jesus called in a loud voice,
"Lazarus, come out!" *John 11:43*

The crowd surely gasped, whether in fear or astonishment.
Others who had died and been miraculously brought back to life
by Jesus—the son of the widow of Nain[31] and the daughter of
Jairus[32]—were revived within hours of their deaths. Not *four days
later,* after their souls had supposedly departed and their bodies
had begun to decay. Never in the history of the world had such a
feat been accomplished.

Still, this was what the sisters of Bethany had longed for,
prayed for, hoped for.

Please, Lord. Even now. Bring him back to us.

The dead man came out, . . . *John 11:44*

Ah, but a dead man no more! Lazarus was alive. Moving and
breathing. "Quickened by hidden grace within," Augustine said.[33]
Lazarus did exactly what the Master asked him and empowered
him to do. He came forth, called from death to life.

. . . his hands and feet wrapped with strips of linen, and
a cloth around his face. *John 11:44*

How Lazarus moved when he could neither walk nor see
properly was all part of the miracle. One more task and his re-
stored body would be set free.

Jesus said to them, "Take off the grave clothes and let
him go." *John 11:44*

This was Mary and Martha's cue to run to their brother's side. Hadn't they dressed him for burial? Who better to "loose him, and let him go" (KJV)! Mourning turned into dancing, and grief gave way to joy. The brother lost to them had been returned, and God was glorified, just as Jesus had promised.

Now for the best part. A large number of onlookers who were counted among the lost that day were found. Those who were dead in sin were brought to life in Christ.

> Therefore many of the Jews who had come to visit
> Mary, and had seen what Jesus did, believed in him.
> *John 11:45*

They'd followed Mary to the tomb and in doing so met the Lord. Is there anything more exciting, more thrilling than watching people we know come to know the One we love? Because of the miracle they'd witnessed, they "trusted in him" (CJB) and "put their faith in him" (CEV). Jesus said He was the Son of God, and now they believed Him.

Hallelujah! God be praised!

To be honest, I'd love to end our story here with lives changed and hearts strengthened and Lazarus walking in newness of life. But it was not the end, especially not for Jesus. His journey through the heart of darkness was only beginning.

Indeed, not everyone who saw what happened that day believed. Instead, they talked.

> But some of them went to the Pharisees and told them
> what Jesus had done. *John 11:46*

Troublemakers. In every time and every place, they're waiting in the wings. Gossiping. Whispering. Scheming. They may not know the source of their evil plans, but Jesus does. "From their callous hearts comes iniquity; their evil imaginations have no limits."[34]

Jesus was loved by many yet feared by those in power. The chief priests and the Pharisees grumbled, "If we let him go on like this, everyone will believe in him."[35] A wonderful plan. But it wasn't the Pharisees' plan.

> So from that day on they plotted to take his life.
> *John 11:53*

And so it began. The path to Calvary.

Three

Lo! I come with joy to do the Master's
    blessed will;
Him in outward works pursue, and serve
    His pleasure still;
Faithful to my Lord's commands, **I still
    would choose the better part,**
Serve with careful Martha's hands, and
    loving Mary's heart.

—CHARLES WESLEY, "LO! I COME
WITH JOY TO DO," 1747

I Still Would Choose
the Better Part

*C*hange stirred the air, like the desert wind sweeping up grains of sand. Invisible, but palpable.

Lazarus, once in a grave, was now alive. Jesus, very much alive, would soon be in a grave, though the disciples could not fathom the possibility. When Jesus told them He would be delivered into the hands of men, they didn't understand what that meant.[1]

But I believe Mary of Bethany understood.

Jesus may have assured her He would return to their village so she could take solace in knowing she'd not seen the last of Him. Until then, He needed to lie low. His hour had not yet come.

> Therefore Jesus no longer moved about publicly among the people of Judea. *John 11:54*

"Because of this plot against him" (CEV), Jesus "stopped his public ministry and left Jerusalem" (TLB). It wasn't safe for Him to circulate, let alone teach "openly among the Jews" (AMP) and especially among the Jewish leaders.

Jesus was neither afraid of them nor avoiding them. He was simply acting according to His Father's will. Whenever my prayers are answered with a firm directive to wait, I remind myself that even Jesus had times of waiting, and more than once He did so in a desolate place.

> Instead he withdrew to a region near the wilderness, to a village called Ephraim, . . . *John 11:54*

A forsaken cluster of dwellings, this "small town known as Ephraim" (VOICE) stood in the "countryside on the edge of the desert" (PHILLIPS).

> . . . where he stayed with his disciples. *John 11:54*

They'd been on the road together for several seasons. And not just men. Whenever "Jesus traveled about from one town and village to another, . . . the Twelve were with him, and also some women."[2] Yes, female believers. Some are named in Scripture, some are not, but it's clear these generous sisters of the faith played an important role in the life of Jesus and His disciples, "helping to support them out of their own means."[3] More about these women as Holy Week unfolds. For now we'll count them among His followers waiting in Ephraim.

Jesus "secluded himself there" (MSG) and "set up camp" (VOICE). John's gospel provides no further details and instead presses on with the story, with Palm Sunday on the horizon.

> When it was almost time for the Jewish Passover, . . .
> *John 11:55*

We sense the excitement mounting. The "pasch of the Jews" (DRA), an annual festival celebrating "God's rescue of Israel from Egypt" (EXB), was circled on everyone's calendar.

> . . . many went up from the country to Jerusalem . . .
> *John 11:55*

A hundred thousand people definitely qualifies as *many*![4] Catching their first glimpse of the Holy City, pilgrims often broke into song and danced with joyous abandon. They poured through the gates of Jerusalem, overflowed into Bethany and other surrounding villages, and set up tent cities in the valleys below Jerusalem, with their four-legged beasts in tow. Some animals carried supplies. Others were chosen to be sacrificed,[5] lambs in particular. During the Passover festival more than a quarter million lambs would be laid on the altar.[6] A sobering reminder of what was to come.

Even the word *sacrifice* chills us to the bone as we consider our Savior laying down His life as the "ultimate Passover Lamb."[7] Yet He *gave* His life, and He did so willingly. "For the joy set before him he endured the cross."[8] And fathom this: *we* were the joy set before Him, beloved. We're the reason for this season of grace. However dark the days ahead, the Lord never lost sight of His goal: our redemption.

While Jesus waited in Ephraim, the pilgrims in Jerusalem got "ready for the Feast" (MSG), which meant finding a place to bathe and "hallow themselves" (WYC).

> . . . for their ceremonial cleansing before the Passover.
> *John 11:55*

People arrived several days early so they could go through the "special washing that would make them pure" (NIrV). After they spent time in one of the ceremonial baths near the Temple Mount, they entered the courts and began celebrating in earnest—eating, dancing, singing, drinking, and, of course, talking about anyone who wasn't there. Some things never change.

> They kept looking for Jesus, . . . *John 11:56*

The ubiquitous *they*. The crowd, the horde. "People were looking for Jesus, hoping to catch a glimpse of Him in the city" (VOICE). Not because they loved Him, but because they were curious about Him and so "gossiped in the Temple" (TLB).

"Did you hear about Lazarus?"

"Who hasn't!"

"Yes, but have you *seen* him? Is he truly alive?"

"The better question is, was he truly *dead*?"

"Jesus of Nazareth said he was. Though we haven't seen Him either . . ."

> . . . and as they stood in the temple courts they asked one another, "What do you think? Isn't he coming to the festival at all?" *John 11:56*

Considering the controversy about back-to-life Lazarus, people knew it would be risky for Jesus to show up in Jerusalem. "Surely he will not come to the festival, will he?" (GNT).

> . . . the chief priests and the Pharisees had given orders that anyone who found out where Jesus was should report it . . . *John 11:57*

Their ruling power alone was incentive for people to heed their "commandment" (ASV) and "report him immediately" (TLB). There is no mention of a cash reward, but you know the idea must have crossed people's minds as easily as silver crossed their palms.

The priests and Pharisees certainly didn't hide their intentions.

> . . . so that they might arrest him. *John 11:57*

First, they'd have to "catch him" (WE). The time had come for Jesus to leave the safety of Ephraim and embrace His future and ours.

> Six days before the Passover, . . . *John 12:1*

On our calendars this is the day before Palm Sunday, the day the Eastern Orthodox Church calls Lazarus Saturday, bearing witness to the power of Christ over death.[9] Whether Lazarus had stepped from his tomb a week ago or months earlier—the exact date is not mentioned in Scripture—Jesus knew it was time for Him to go forward.

> . . . Jesus came to Bethany, where Lazarus lived, whom Jesus had raised from the dead. *John 12:1*

These are facts we already know, confirmed again in John's gospel. No detail is insignificant. The time, the place, the people— they all matter. Our God cares about everything and everyone. Nothing escapes Him.

Mary was prepared for Jesus's return to Bethany. So was her

brother, and Martha was present too, but—this is unexpected—
they gathered in a home other than theirs.

> . . . Jesus was in Bethany in the home of Simon the
> Leper, . . . *Matthew 26:6*

Maybe Simon's house was bigger and could accommodate
more people. If so, it was a good thing, because in addition to
all the special guests who were invited, Jesus arrived with His
disciples—"perhaps a dozen men and an equal number of
women."[10]

Simon was a common name, but this man's health history
made him a standout. He "had had *tzara'at*" (CJB), the Hebrew
word for "leprosy."[11] The past perfect tense assures us Simon was
"no longer the victim of that dreadful disease."[12] Otherwise, the
whole dinner party would have been "violating Mosaic law."[13]

Their host was still called Simon the Leper in the same way
the righteous mother of Boaz was referred to as "Rahab the prostitute"[14] centuries after her conversion. Old labels serve as a lasting
reminder of God's grace. That's why I call myself a Former Bad
Girl, lest I ever forget His goodness and mercy.

By opening his home, Simon the Former Leper made his
gratitude known.

> Here a dinner was given in Jesus' honor. *John 12:2*

Not just any evening supper of lentils and leeks, this was a
"banquet" (TLB), a chance to honor the Lord with a fine meal even
as His enemies plotted against Him. Did the dinner guests sense
the tension in the air? Were they whispering at the door, exchang-

ing glances around the room? Or were they too busy noshing on pressed figs and poached fish?

It's easy to lose sight of eternity when a plate of food lands in front of you.

Martha served, . . . *John 12:2*

Naturally. Serving was what Martha did best. The house was surely filled with the pungent aromas of freshly baked bread, well-seasoned meats, and grains roasted in olive oil—all her favorite recipes.

Martha humbly "waited on the party" (PHILLIPS), further proof of her maturing faith. This time she didn't ask others to help her or complain to Jesus about her work load. Instead, she served "without care and distraction" and with "no more murmuring at Mary."[15] Her brother was well and whole, and Jesus was back from Ephraim. Martha's soul was well satisfied.

. . . while Lazarus was among those reclining at the table with him. *John 12:2*

The friends who had mourned Lazarus's passing now came to pay homage to the One who had raised him. When Lazarus joined the Lord, he didn't pull up a chair, since "it was customary to eat formal meals while reclining around a low table" (EXB).

So awkward. Imagine partaking of a meal while stretched out on the floor—or, in wealthier homes, on a low couch—propped up on your left elbow and eating with your right hand. I'd be wearing my food from shoulder to shin. But Jesus, the honored guest, was adept at such customs.

With His feet exposed rather than tucked under a table, nothing stood between Mary of Bethany and the Lord she longed to worship. And so we find her right where we'd expect her to be. Kneeling at His feet. Again.

The last time we were with Mary, her faith had seemed to falter momentarily, and her hope had dissolved into tears. "Lord, if you had been here . . ." This evening's act of worship was perhaps a means of seeking His forgiveness and certainly a deep expression of her belief in Him. Mary's "unspoken but eloquent witness now stands worthily alongside her sister Martha's wonderful confession."[16]

It does indeed. Watch this.

> Then Mary took about a pint of pure nard, . . .
> *John 12:3*

Make no mistake. This was Mary of Bethany, not the unnamed prostitute described in Luke 7, who had also anointed Jesus's feet. Their stories are often confused, but they were two different people on two different occasions.

One is called "a sinful woman,"[17] yet Mary of Bethany "is never referred to as a sinner in any of the accounts of her."[18] Also, the unnamed woman anointed His feet "a year before the crucifixion in the area around Galilee."[19] But this scene recorded by John took place in Bethany, some seventy or eighty miles south of Galilee, and just six days before the crucifixion. The nearness of the Lord's death is pivotal to this story, for Mary of Bethany and for Him.

How much pure nard did Mary have in her hands? "A twelve-ounce jar" (NLT), the typical size of our modern soda can. It's also called a "pound" (ASV) in Scripture, since a Roman pound was about twelve ounces.[20] However we measure her perfume, it was "an extraordinary amount" (CEB).

Each year for Christmas my husband, Bill, presents me with a one-ounce bottle of my favorite perfume, Estée Lauder's Beautiful. If I limit myself to a few careful squirts a day, I can make a single ounce last a full year. At that rate Mary could have used her "pure liquid nard" (AMPC) for *a dozen years.*

But wearing this perfume was not what Mary had in mind that evening.

Her "oil of spikenard" (CJB) was made from the roots and hairy stems of a flowering plant in the valerian family,[21] crushed and distilled into an essential oil with an amber color, an intense scent, and a very thick consistency. Now we see why some translators call it an "ointment" (ASV) and others a "fragrant oil" (EXB).

Bet they'd all agree on a name: Eau de Pricey.

> . . . an expensive perfume; . . . *John 12:3*

Imported from northern India, the oil was "precious" (ASV) and "rare" (AMPC) and therefore "very costly" (KJV). The last thing we would do with something so valuable is pour it onto a man's feet.

But we're not Mary.

> She broke the jar . . . *Mark 14:3*

Whether the Bible calls it a "vase" (CEB), a "vial" (NASB), a "special sealed jar" (NIrV), or a "box of alabaster" (WYC), Mary broke it open. The only way to release this perfume from its "thin-necked alabaster flask" was by "snapping off the neck,"[22] so the container could never be used again.

Mary intended to release it all and save nothing for herself. Though Mark's gospel calls it "a beautiful flask,"[23] only the contents mattered, and Mary of Bethany wanted to sacrifice every fragrant drop.

We can be sure Mary paid no attention to the raisin cakes on the table or the oil lamps scattered around the room. She was looking at the One she loved as she held the broken flask in her trembling hands.

For You, Lord. All for You.

> . . . she poured it on Jesus' feet . . . *John 12:3*

Ounce after ounce drenched His skin, soaked the hem of His garment, pooled on the floor around His heels. With the fragrant perfume running through her fingers, Mary "anointed and massaged Jesus's feet" (MSG) right there in front of God and everybody. Rather than a royal or priestly anointing, her ministrations were about hospitality and care,[24] "an act of love to a living person."[25]

Friend, it was scandalous. And glorious.

Should you read in Matthew's gospel that Mary poured her perfume "on his head,"[26] don't be concerned. Since "the normal procedure was to anoint the head, not the feet,"[27] Mary may have done that first. But what John found worth noting in his gospel was that she anointed the Lord's *feet.* It was more unusual, more distinctive—and far more humbling. Anoint His head? Of course. But His feet? Oh my.

Was this aromatic substance cool to the touch or warm? Sticky or silky? Only Jesus and Mary knew how it felt. But everyone knew what it meant. *I love You, I honor You, I worship and adore You.*

Mary of Bethany was not one to use words when actions spoke louder. She, who once sat at the Lord's feet to learn[28] and fell at His feet to weep,[29] now knelt at His feet with "queenlike nobleness,"[30] offering a priceless gift. And she wasn't finished.

Gratitude and reverence brought her to her knees. Love drew her closer still. Following the same path as her perfume, her dark hair spilled across His feet.

> . . . and wiped his feet with her hair. *John 12:3*

Oh, Lord.

No words.

The original Greek simply reads "the hair of her with the feet of him."[31] Yes, that's it. Her hair. His feet. But there's so much more between the lines. God's Word tells us "if a woman has long hair, it is her glory,"[32] meaning her hair is closely tied to her sense of "self-worth and self-respect."[33] Mary was quietly letting go of self: of her longing to be looked up to, of her desire to be attractive, of her need to be liked.

This devout follower, this beloved sister, used her long hair to dry a man's feet—the "lowest job for the lowliest servant."[34] Human opinion meant nothing to her. Though it was "against Jewish convention for a hostess to appear in the presence of men with unbound hair,"[35] there she was. Unbound.

Mary cared nothing about convention and everything about Jesus.

Her perfume wasn't the only thing she sacrificed. Mary laid her whole being before Him: her pride, her reputation, her social standing, her clean hands, her pure heart. She asked nothing of Him, sought no sign of approval, begged for no favors. Confident of His love and acceptance, she simply gave, expecting nothing in return.

She anointed Him in silence, an especially sacred manner of worship. I suspect the roomful of men was silent too. Washing a guest's feet with water was commonplace. But *this* was "the most lavish, extravagant act of love ever shown to Jesus while he lived on earth. No one had ever done such a thing."[36] Until Mary of Bethany.

The only time I witnessed a foot washing, the feet were mine. I was ministering in Thailand with a group of sisters in Christ who had traveled there for the same reason I had—to show God's love to hundreds of young women trapped in the sex trade. On our last day in Bangkok, the team gathered to reflect on all God had accomplished. Then, to my surprise, the woman in charge asked me to sit in the center of the group so they could minister to me as well. By washing my feet.

Gulp.

I couldn't refuse—how rude!—but I wasn't at all comfortable. I sat there, not knowing where to look, what to say, how to feel. These were my sisters, my friends, kneeling at my feet. Should I thank them? Bless them? Apologize to them?

One by one they obediently washed my feet. I wish I could tell you I enjoyed it. Mostly, I was embarrassed. I wanted to say, "Now let me wash *your* feet." That seemed more fair, more biblical. But that's not what was happening. So I nodded my thanks, hoping I looked grateful, penitent—something.

To this day I don't know what my traveling sisters gained from that exercise, but I can tell you what I learned: it takes a great deal of humility to receive such a personal, hands-on gift. I also discovered that beneath my thin veneer of discomfort was a thick layer of pride. I didn't like being singled out. I didn't like all the attention. And I especially didn't like people touching my feet. In short, I was out of my depth and ill prepared to be honored.

But Jesus? He gladly received Mary's fragrant, loving gift. Welcomed her touch. Celebrated her sacrifice. Breathed in the rich aroma of a soul set free.

> And the house was filled with the fragrance of the perfume. *John 12:3*

The aroma carried far and wide since "the evocative scent of spikenard could be smelled up to half a mile away."[37] Their neighbors in Bethany no doubt lifted their heads and sniffed the evening air.

Mary's private devotion had become a public display of affection, though she was probably unaware of it. Just as when we're standing in church, our hearts and eyes lifted up, our minds focused entirely on Him as if no one else were in the sanctuary.

Alas, such tender scenes seldom last. The world intrudes, makes demands, even protests.

> But one of his disciples, Judas Iscariot, who was later to betray him, objected, . . . *John 12:4*

John, an eyewitness, wasn't afraid to name names. He described how Judas, the future betrayer, "complained" (CEB) about Mary's actions. This man, "who would later hand Jesus over to his enemies" (ERV), was a disciple in name only—"not one of their nature, but only one of their number."[38] Since Judas worshiped his silver far more than his Savior, he found Mary's actions distasteful, disgraceful, and, above all, wasteful—and didn't hesitate to say so.

> "Why wasn't this perfume sold and the money given to the poor?" *John 12:5*

We hear the unrighteous anger, the cruel tone, the sharp accusation in those words. "How could she pour out this vast amount of fine oil?" (VOICE).

Concerns are often raised about any great expense related to worship. A beautiful stained-glass window. A sterling-silver Communion cup. A carefully embroidered kneeling cushion. "Waste of time and money," some might protest. "Couldn't it be better spent?"

If such gifts are designed to impress other worshipers, then, yes, the high cost should be questioned. But if they're made with love and laid at the feet of the Savior to give honor and glory to Him alone, are they not a precious and worthy sacrifice?

When Judas grumbled, "Why did we not sell it?" (WE), I wish someone had shot back, "Because it wasn't yours to sell, buddy." Mary's perfume was of great worth. What mattered to Judas was the street value.

> "It was worth a year's wages." *John 12:5*

We knew it was costly. Judas, being Judas, tarnished the gift by stating the price. "Three hundred silver coins" (CEV), he said bluntly. "A full year's pay" (ERV) for "an ordinary workman" (AMPC). In today's economy that's roughly thirty thousand dollars.[39] For a bottle of perfume.

I'm left with a hard question. Could I give an entire year's salary to Jesus? Could I pour my earnings onto His body and into the ground, knowing every penny was gone as soon as it left the container?

I'm starting to sound like Judas. *It seems so impractical, Lord. So careless.*

God's Word quickly undoes that kind of thinking. "And what do you benefit if you gain the whole world but lose your own soul?"[40]

We know the answer. Sadly, Judas did not.

> He did not say this because he cared about the poor but because he was a thief; as keeper of the money bag, he used to help himself to what was put into it. *John 12:6*

For Judas it all came down to money. One might ask how in the world he ended up in charge of "the purse of the Twelve" (AMPC), considering he was a "robber" (NLV) and took "money from the common pot at every opportunity" (VOICE).

Jesus knew the man's dark heart. Why did He allow him in His inner circle? Because Judas, with his "deadly sins of greed and covetousness,"[41] had a part to play in God's redemption plan. So did Mary of Bethany, the opposite of Judas in every way. She was generous. Judas was greedy. She remained loyal to the Lord. Judas betrayed Him. She knew what it meant to worship. Judas didn't have a clue. And he wasn't the only one.

Some of those present were saying indignantly to one another, "Why this waste of perfume?" *Mark 14:4*

More specifically, "the disciples"[42] saw what Mary did and became "angry" (ICB) and "upset" (NCV), chiming in with their own heated question: "What is the point of such wicked waste of perfume?" (PHILLIPS). Even Jesus's own men couldn't see past the material loss to appreciate the gracious gain of her worship and sacrifice. From their viewpoint Mary's anointing served no purpose *because it did not benefit them.* An ugly attitude familiar to us all: "What's in it for me?" If we're told, "Not a thing," we don't always handle the news well.

And they rebuked her harshly. *Mark 14:5*

They didn't just wag their fingers at her. They "scolded" (CEB) and "criticized" (GNT); they "censured and reproved" (AMPC). With no concern for her feelings, "they told the woman what a bad thing she had done" (ERV). Poor Mary of Bethany! To share something holy and then to be treated cruelly, not by strangers, but by those who knew her and claimed to know Christ.

Jesus offered a rebuke of His own, aimed not at Mary but at the disciples.

"Leave her alone," Jesus replied. *John 12:7*

Can I just say, *I love this.* Jesus rushed to her defense without Mary needing to say a word. "Don't stop her" (ERV), Jesus told His men, brooking no argument.

Mark's gospel captures more of the Lord's conversation with the disciples, beginning with a pointed question.

"Why are you bothering her?" *Mark 14:6*

Heated tempers must have cooled at once. Gazes were surely averted, and voices stilled. "Instead of condemning her, they should have commended her."[43] That task fell to Jesus, and commend her He did.

"She has done a beautiful thing to me." *Mark 14:6*

Beautiful. That's exactly what the original Greek means. Her actions were also "praiseworthy and noble" (AMPC), "excellent" (EXB), and "wonderfully significant" (MSG). But beautiful goes deeper. It has little to do with appearance and everything to do with a woman's character: her integrity, her charity, her sincerity.

Because Mary's deed was beautiful, so was she. Her beauty was revealed in brokenness. Only when the jar was snapped in two, and her pride with it, was her sweet perfume released.

Perhaps by divine revelation Mary of Bethany knew what awaited Jesus in six short days. While she sat at His feet, if she "read the secret of His pain,"[44] the Lord may have revealed to her that in the very near future His body would be broken and His blood would be spilled. Certainly the next words He spoke made that clear.

"It was intended that she should save this perfume for the day of my burial." *John 12:7*

Mary had done as God intended, saving her precious ointment for months, perhaps years, uncertain as to what end. On a
vastly smaller scale, I've done that, and I'll bet you have too—set
aside a special gift, uncertain whom it was for, and waited for the
right time and the right person to give it to.

Some scholars interpret Jesus's words to mean He asked her to
save some perfume for His actual burial. But she'd broken the
seal. She'd poured it all out and held nothing back. Besides, as
we'll discover later, the women who hurried to the tomb on that
Sunday morning had purchased fresh spices for His body.[45]

"It was right for her to save this perfume for today" (ERV),
Jesus said, "anticipating and honoring the day of my burial" (MSG).
Jesus was preparing His heart, even as Mary of Bethany was preparing His body. Death was coming. The reality of it had "entered
deep into the heart of Mary."[46] Jesus wanted the others to grasp
that truth and see it as clearly as she did.

When Jesus had explained to His followers earlier, "The Son
of Man must suffer many things and . . . be killed and after three
days rise again,"[47] Peter had taken Him aside and rebuked Him,[48]
unwilling to believe that anyone would kill their beloved Teacher.
But Mary of Bethany believed. The proof of her faith now dripped
from her hands, her hair, His feet.

Though she loved her brother, Mary didn't reach for her
spikenard when Lazarus died. Perhaps she'd not purchased it yet
or had already set it aside for the Lord. Certainly the perfume was
hers to give, "not belonging to her brother or sister or to the household, but to herself."[49] It's no sacrifice if someone else bears the
expense.

When our children were small, we'd give them money to put

into the offering plate, hoping to teach them the importance of giving. But they didn't learn about sacrifice until they reached into their own wallets and slipped out a crumpled bill to tuck beneath the others.

Jesus knows all that can be known about sacrifice. He didn't for a moment discount the less fortunate when He told His disciples:

"You will always have the poor among you, . . ."
John 12:8

His words weren't dismissive. They were meant to remind His followers, then and now, to be aware of the poor and to care for them. Their needs must be met, especially in the village of Bethany, meaning "the house of the poor."[50]

". . . and you can help them any time you want."
Mark 14:7

Jesus was urging them to do so, just as He did. "Christ loved the poor, gave himself for the poor, preached the gospel to the poor, and made himself poor that he might make the poor rich."[51]

Once again the word *but* prepares us for a change in direction.

". . . but you will not always have me." *John 12:8*

Another foreshadowing, which probably wafted over the disciples' heads like the fragrant aroma of Mary's perfume. "I won't be with you very long" (TLB), Jesus told them. How I wish we could move in for a closer look at their faces! Were the disciples and other guests surprised? Distressed? Confused?

The Lord didn't pause to explain. He was still talking about Mary's sacrifice and wanted to keep the focus on her. The simplicity of what He said next only enhances its power.

"She did what she could." *Mark 14:8*

Oh, Jesus. How often have I done only what I must instead of all that I could? Help me give like Mary. Help me love like Mary.

Mary of Bethany did what God called and equipped her to do. Give extravagantly. Love abundantly. As Jesus said, "What she could do, she did do" (CJB).

"She poured perfume on my body beforehand to prepare for my burial." *Mark 14:8*

Jesus had all but given up on subtlety. "Before I die" (ERV), He told them plainly, Mary "pre-anointed my body" (MSG) so she could "make Me ready for the grave" (NLV). Could the Lord have been any more forthright? Words like *body* and *burial* were meant to get their attention.

But no protest was raised. No questions were asked. Maybe they assumed He meant someday far away in the sweet by and by. We understand. The impending death of a friend is never easy to accept.

We can almost see Jesus looking at Mary, with the purest kind of love shining in His eyes, as He spoke these words.

"Truly I tell you, wherever the gospel is preached
throughout the world, what she has done will also
be told, in memory of her." *Mark 14:9*

Wow, sister. *Wherever* means *everywhere* since "this gospel of
the kingdom will be preached throughout the whole inhabited
earth."[52] People in all the nations of the world would hear not only
the good news of God's mercy but also the story of a quiet, faith-
filled woman from the village of Bethany who dared to believe
every word Jesus said.

Mary is remembered not for the ointment itself, however aromatic, and not for her generous sacrifice, however impressive, but
for her boundless faith, believing that Jesus would die and rise
again. The disciples rejected the truth at that moment, yet Mary
received it, showing "every evidence of knowing more of His secret power and wisdom than His disciples did."[53] Mary of Bethany both believed and acted upon her beliefs—an indication of
the Holy Spirit at work even before His power was poured out at
Pentecost.

Jesus said, "People will remember what she has done" (CEV).
We remember, Lord. She heard what others did not hear and saw
what others did not see. And for that, Mary of Bethany will never
be forgotten.

Four

All glory, laud and honor, to Thee,
    Redeemer, King,
To Whom the lips of children made sweet
    hosannas ring.
The people of the Hebrews **with palms
    before Thee** went;
Our prayer and praise and anthems before
    Thee we present.

—Translated by John Mason Neale,
"All Glory, Laud and Honor," 1851

With Palms
Before Thee

alms can mean the soft centers of our hands, like Mary of Bethany's palms that touched the feet of Jesus. Or the palms of God, on which He has written our names: "Behold, I have inscribed you on the palms of My hands."[1]

Palms are also tall, graceful plants found throughout Scripture and often used in worship. "You are to take branches from luxuriant trees—from palms, willows and other leafy trees—and rejoice before the LORD your God."[2]

In the next chapter of Jesus's life, both kinds of palms would be used to honor Him, with the waving of branches and the clapping of hands.

> Meanwhile a large crowd of Jews found out that Jesus
> was there and came, . . . *John 12:9*

While Mary wiped His feet dry with her hair, half the known world, it seemed, headed for their village. Not only had the scent of her perfume carried some distance. So had reports of the One she was anointing.

Even without a head count, we know this was a "great multi-tude" (DRA), drawn to Bethany when "word got out among the Jews that he was back in town" (MSG). Rather than the chief priests, these were "common people" (ASV) seeking Jesus out of curiosity and wonder.

> . . . not only because of him but also to see Lazarus, whom he had raised from the dead. *John 12:9*

You *know* this dinner party was the talk of the local villagers. For starters, Jesus was there. So was a healed leper, a world-class aromatherapist, and a man who'd risen from the grave. It was that last one, the dead man walking, who troubled the authorities.

> So the chief priests made plans to kill Lazarus as well, . . . *John 12:10*

Never mind that Lazarus was innocent of any wrongdoing. He served as living proof of the power Jesus commanded. That's why the priests "plotted" (EXB) and "conspired" (WEB), looking for a way "to put Lazarus to death" (NKJV).

In those days it was risky to be friends with Jesus of Nazareth. But Lazarus was past worrying about what people said of him. You can be certain that after the Lord raised him from the dead, Lazarus and his sisters told anyone who would listen that he'd been in a grave for four days and then walked out alive.

Imagine all the mourners from Jerusalem who'd seen Lazarus buried, grieved his passing, and then marveled at his return. With so many eyewitnesses the truth was undeniable. Jesus must be who He said He was: the Son of God, fully capable of resurrecting a dead man.

> . . . for on account of him many of the Jews were going over to Jesus and believing in him. *John 12:11*

From where we're sitting, this is great news—more people "putting their faith in Jesus" (CEV) and "following Him as Savior and Messiah" (AMP). But that's not how the chief priests saw it. They were furious that "many Jews were leaving their own religion" (NLV). The priests didn't understand that Jesus was their long-awaited Anointed One,[3] the central figure in their own prophecies.

Jesus was born to upset the status quo. His ideas were revolutionary, His method of ministry unconventional. Eat with tax collectors? Seek out sinners rather than hang out with the righteous?[4] That approach didn't fly with the religious leaders, who were busily plotting His death.

On the next day[5]—Palm Sunday—our heavenly Father brought His Son one step closer to giving His life in order to guarantee ours. Jesus, still fragrant with Mary's perfume, led His followers toward the Holy City.

> As they approached Jerusalem and came to Bethphage on the Mount of Olives, Jesus sent two disciples, . . . *Matthew 21:1*

Bethphage, a walled village not far from Bethany, was the only place outside the city of Jerusalem where the Sanhedrin held court. One of the duties handled in Bethphage was validating death sentences for rebellious leaders.[6] *Hmm.* Another foreshadowing, another reminder of what lay ahead for Jesus.

Was Mary of Bethany by His side, joining the women who traveled with Him—Mary Magdalene, Joanna, Susanna, and the others?[7] Surely Mary of Bethany "could not have stayed in her home,"[8] not when her Savior's life was threatened. It seems likely that she would have wanted to keep Him in sight as long as possible and that the Lord would have welcomed her quiet support.

As Jesus and His followers came closer to Jerusalem, He sent two of them ahead with a special assignment. Why two men instead of one? For protection as they pressed through the crowds and for credibility when they presented Jesus's request.

> . . . saying to them, "Go to the village ahead of you,
> and at once you will find a donkey tied there, with
> her colt by her. Untie them and bring them to me."
> *Matthew 21:2*

By then the disciples had grown accustomed to such foreknowledge from the Lord. No need to stroll through town and knock on doors when "Jesus arranged for the ride."[9] Just inside the gate they would "immediately find a donkey tethered there with its colt" (cjb). Luke added a detail in his gospel—"which no one has ever ridden."[10]

Jesus told the two disciples to "loose" (asv) the donkeys—not steal them—and have an answer ready if they were questioned.

> "If anyone says anything to you, say that the Lord needs
> them, and he will send them right away." *Matthew 21:3*

It's unclear from the original Greek whether Jesus was telling His men that the owner would quickly send the animals or that He would return them ASAP. Either way, the result was the same: donkeys on demand.

Everything went according to plan with "no trouble" (TLB). Naturally.

> This took place to fulfill what was spoken through the prophet:
>
> "Say to Daughter Zion,
>   'See, your king comes to you,
> gentle and riding on a donkey,
>   and on a colt, the foal of a donkey.'"
>   *Matthew 21:4–5*

Why bring the little one? Practically speaking, mother donkeys never leave their offspring behind, and foals never let their mothers get out of sight. Spiritually speaking, Jesus honored every prophecy, knowing "not the smallest letter or stroke shall pass from the Law until all is accomplished."[11] Every detail was just as "the prophet Zechariah had long since foretold" (VOICE). And Zechariah wrote those prophetic words[12] more than *five centuries* before the Messiah rode into Jerusalem.

The fact that Jesus was "riding a donkey rather than a war-horse"[13] alerted the crowd that this was no ordinary man. Some *ten centuries* earlier Solomon mounted a mule and rode into Gihon, where Zadok the priest and Nathan the prophet anointed him as king over Israel, according to David's instructions.[14] Now this Son of David was preparing to make the same kind of entry.

Not as a conqueror on a horse, but as a rightful king entering in peace.

Donkeys by their nature are associated with gentleness and intelligence. Rather than being stubborn, they have a keen sense of danger and proceed only when the path is safe.[15] God's Word makes it clear that the Lord will "come to you meekly"[16] and "make your paths straight."[17] He enters our hearts the same way. Gently, yet with sure footing and great strength.

> The disciples went and did as Jesus had instructed them.
> *Matthew 21:6*

No questions were asked. They simply did His bidding. The owner, too, was obedient, releasing the two animals with haste.

> They brought the donkey and the colt and placed their
> cloaks on them for Jesus to sit on. *Matthew 21:7*

Jesus could hardly ride both animals at once, but perhaps the "young donkey" (ERV) carried the extra garments on its back, while Jesus mounted the mother donkey and continued His journey.

> The great crowd that had come for the festival heard
> that Jesus was on his way to Jerusalem. *John 12:12*

With the Jewish Sabbath having ended the evening before, the streets of the Holy City were overflowing with festival goers. News quickly traveled the scant two miles from Bethany to Jerusalem and "swept through the city" (TLB). *He is coming.*

> They took palm branches and went out to meet him, . . .
> *John 12:13*

As it happens, palms are flowering plants that have no branches—or tree rings, for that matter. What they do have is huge leaves, perfect for waving as a "symbol of the nation of Israel" (EXB) and "in homage to Him as King" (AMP).

> When he came near the place where the road goes down
> the Mount of Olives, . . . *Luke 19:37*

A fairly steep road meandered down the hillside. Olive trees, with their twisted trunks and silvery leaves, flanked the path. The city of Jerusalem rose on the other side of the Kidron Valley, dominating the view.

As Jesus "rode through the crowds mounted on this small beast,"[18] He was surrounded by hands holding out palms, hearts holding out hope, faces filled with anticipation. Men, women, and children tried to catch a glimpse of Him. Can you feel the heat of the sun, see the dust rising from the ground, hear the shouts of adoration?

> . . . the whole crowd of disciples began joyfully to praise
> God in loud voices for all the miracles they had seen: . . .
> *Luke 19:37*

Everyone joined in the excitement, those "that went ahead of him and those that followed."[19] This is what they shouted:

> "Hosanna to the Son of David!" *Matthew 21:9*

"Blessed is he who comes in the name of the Lord!"
Matthew 21:9

"Peace in heaven and glory in the highest!" *Luke 19:38*

"Blessed is the king of Israel!" *John 12:13*

What a cacophony of sound as they all "spoke with a loud voice" (NLV), "cried out" (NKJV), and "cheered" (MSG).[20] On that Sunday in Jerusalem, enthusiasm for the Messiah was at a fever pitch.

Hosanna was "an Aramaic cry to God for salvation, which became a shout of praise."[21] And the words "Blessed is he who comes in the name of the LORD"[22] came straight from their sacred psalms. A thousand years earlier people had shouted, "Long live King Solomon!"[23] In fact, their rejoicing was so great "the ground shook with the sound."[24] The collective history of Israel converged on a dusty road leading to Jerusalem that day, right down to the volume of their praise.

But this teeming throng didn't simply worship with their voices. They made it personal, giving Him the shirts off their backs.

A very large crowd spread their cloaks on the road, . . .
Matthew 21:8

People willingly sacrificed their outer garments, knowing the fabric would be trampled by countless pairs of feet, in order to give Jesus "a royal welcome" (MSG). They "threw down their coats" (TLB) and "carpeted the road with their clothing" (CJB), while the poor who could not spare their cloaks "cut leaves from the palm trees and put them on the road" (we).

This wasn't peer pressure or mob mentality. This was the presence of the Son of God lifting them to a place they'd never been before. They had to respond, had to honor Him as their king, had to show Him what was in their hearts, had to worship Him.

Has the Lord's presence ever washed over you like that, catching you by surprise? Perhaps you found yourself singing louder, clapping harder, lifting your hands, or rising to your feet. You weren't worrying about what others were thinking. Your total focus was on the One who calls His people to "worship the LORD in the splendor of his holiness."[25] You were fully aware of His presence. He was *there.* A sense of peace, of rightness flooded your soul.

Worship isn't a task. Worship is a response.

That day in Jerusalem the people of God were worshiping Him with all their might. Not only honoring an unseen God in heaven, but also praising an incarnate God on a donkey, close enough to touch.

Even so, those who knew Him best were taken aback by the crowd's reaction.

> At first his disciples did not understand all this. *John 12:16*

Such confusion was standard procedure for the disciples—always two steps behind, always asking foolish questions. They had eyes to see but refused to look. Ears to hear but refused to listen. They didn't know "what was happening" (erv), didn't realize "this was a fulfillment of prophecy" (tlb).

Some of us are in the same predicament. We study the Bible

yet find it hard to believe everything we read. The Greek word translated "understand" means "to come to know, recognize, perceive."[26] This knowledge isn't something we're born with. God reveals His truth to us once our hearts are prepared to receive it.

The day would come when His disciples understood. But it was not this day.

> Only after Jesus was glorified did they realize that these things had been written about him and that these things had been done to him. *John 12:16*

For the disciples, truth finally found its mark after Jesus returned to heaven, when they discovered that "everything had happened exactly as the Scriptures said it would" (cev). From that point on, the disciples were willing to die for what they believed. Jesus knew that epiphany would come for them, even as He knows when it will come for us.

Meanwhile, many who'd witnessed the miracle of Lazarus walking out of his grave were eager to tell others.

> Now the crowd that was with him when he called Lazarus from the tomb and raised him from the dead continued to spread the word. *John 12:17*

For them, seeing was believing. They "gave testimony" (dra) and shared their "eyewitness accounts" (msg), creating more excitement in Jerusalem.

> Many people, because they had heard that he had performed this sign, went out to meet him. *John 12:18*

As more of the crowd "heard about this mighty miracle" (TLB), they flooded the road to Jerusalem until their numbers "swelled to a welcoming parade" (MSG), and their shouts of adoration filled the air.

You can guess who wasn't pleased to be on the sidelines watching all this.

> Some of the Pharisees in the crowd said to Jesus,
> "Teacher, rebuke your disciples!" *Luke 19:39*

"Scold" (CEB) them for what? Speaking the truth? Praising their king? Did they find His followers too loud? "Make your disciples stop shouting!" (CEV). Or did they think the people were too rowdy? "Get your disciples under control!" (MSG). No, what infuriated the Pharisees were the "Messianic praises" (AMP).

Jesus finally had enough.

Though He was known for His humility, He was also the One through whom God "made the universe"[27] and the One who sustains "all things by his powerful word."[28] With the supreme authority invested in Him, Jesus put these hypocrites in their place.

> "I tell you," he replied, "if they keep quiet, the stones
> will cry out." *Luke 19:40*

Those "stones along the road" (NLT)? Those inanimate rocks? They would "scream,"[29] Jesus told the Pharisees, and "shout!" (CJB) and "burst into cheers!" (NLT) if His disciples remained silent. Think of Isaiah's description of a day when "the mountains and hills will burst into song . . . and all the trees of the field will clap their hands."[30] If J. R. R. Tolkien can imagine giant trees walking about Middle-earth, think what our God can and will do in the real world!

The Pharisees had no clever comeback for screaming stones.

> So the Pharisees said to one another, "See, this is getting us nowhere." *John 12:19*

These "proud religious law-keepers" (NLV) grumbled among themselves, "Our plan is not working" (ERV). In fact, "not succeeding at all" (GNT). One of the Pharisees must have been in charge of their social media, because he complained, "Look, we are losing followers" (NLV). Exasperated, the others shook their heads. "There is nothing that can be done!" (CEV).

> "Look how the whole world has gone after him!" *John 12:19*

Watching hundreds of Jews praising a destitute man on a donkey, the Pharisees surely wondered what this teacher could possibly offer his followers. Yet it was clear: "Everyone is following Jesus!" (NLV).

> As he approached Jerusalem and saw the city, . . .
> *Luke 19:41*

Jesus lifted His head to gaze up at the Holy City, capped with the "gleaming snowy mountain of the Temple,"[31] and was undone.

. . . he wept over it . . . Luke 19:41

"His eye affected his heart, and his heart his eye again."[32] Once more Jesus cried. As the Son of Man, His human heart was breaking. First His friend Lazarus and now a whole city of people were trapped in the grip of death, unaware and unprepared. All around Him people were shouting and rejoicing.

But not Jesus. He wept.

Did His disciples notice His tears? Was Mary of Bethany close enough to hear His lament?

> *. . . and [Jesus] said, "If you, even you, had only known on this day what would bring you peace . . ."*
> *Luke 19:42*

We think we know "what is needed for *shalom*" (CJB)—the love of our parents, the love of our spouses, the love of our children, the love of our friends. All are welcome sources of comfort, but they do not bring the kind of peace Jesus spoke of that day. We believe if we had more money, more security, and more freedom, then peace would follow. But anyone who has those things will tell you they are not enough.

Jesus alone provides everlasting peace.

"Ah, if you only knew, even at this eleventh hour, on what your peace depends" (PHILLIPS), He said. Then and now it depends on knowing Him, believing in Him, and trusting Him.

> *". . . —but now it is hidden from your eyes."*
> *Luke 19:42*

Why didn't the city that He loved see the truth? Because Jerusalem was looking in the wrong direction. Its citizens turned to people, possessions, and power, even though none of them brought peace. "You cannot see it!" (GNT), Jesus said, if only to Himself. "For if thou haddest known, thou shouldest weep also" (WYC).

Only Jesus wept that day, while Jerusalem prepared to throw a party.

He likely entered the city through the southern gate near the Pool of Siloam,[33] where He'd once healed a blind man.[34] Now it seemed all Jerusalem had gone blind.

> When Jesus entered Jerusalem, the whole city
> was stirred and asked, "Who is this?" *Matthew*
> *21:10*

These weren't the people who had initially run out to meet Him but the rest of Jerusalem, who were only now noticing "this strange parade" (VOICE). The Greek word for "stirred" means they were "thrown into an uproar" (GNT) of noise and confusion, as "a shock ran through the whole city" (PHILLIPS). People were asking one another, "What's going on here?" (MSG) and "Who is this!?!" (OJB).

Visitors from distant Babylonia and Crete, who'd not heard of Jesus, were understandably anxious. Jerusalem was at its most crowded and dangerous during festivals, which is one reason Pontius Pilate came from coastal Caesarea Maritima to supervise the Passover.[35]

The Lord's followers were quick to respond to the question "Who is this man?" (ERV).

> The crowds answered, "This is Jesus, the prophet from
> Nazareth in Galilee." *Matthew 21:11*

How proud they were of their Teacher, "the One Who speaks for God" (NLV)! They didn't hesitate to mention His small hometown, even though Nathanael once said, "Nazareth! Can anything good come from there?"[36] Yes, it can. Goodness itself came from there, brought into the world by Mary of Nazareth, the mother of Jesus.

We're not told if she was present on Palm Sunday, though the Bible informs us Mary came to Jerusalem every year for the Passover,[37] despite the long and arduous journey south from Galilee. We also know she was at the cross on Good Friday. So it's no stretch to imagine her by His side now among the growing group of women who called Him Lord.

Mary had no doubt shared with them the story of a Passover long ago when Jesus was a boy on the cusp of manhood. After a week in Jerusalem, she and Joseph had joined the throng of pilgrims returning to Galilee, not realizing that Jesus wasn't with them. On such journeys families divided into two groups—women and children in one, men and older boys in the other.[38] At twelve, Jesus was free to travel in either group. Or, as it turned out, in neither group.

When they couldn't find Jesus among their relatives and friends, Mary and Joseph hurried back to Jerusalem, likely blaming themselves. Who left behind a child in a crowded city? After three days they found him in the temple courts, sitting among the teachers as if He belonged there.

"Why were you searching for me?"[39] Jesus had said. "Didn't you know I had to be in my Father's house?"[40]

Even then Mary hadn't grasped the truth.[41] Her son didn't mean their house in Nazareth, and He wasn't talking about His earthly father, Joseph. That day long ago in Jerusalem she'd caught a glimpse of the man He would become. Though she didn't fully understand Him—what mother could?—she fully loved Him. She realized her son "was on a mission, and she couldn't get in his way."[42] But she could support Him, believe in Him, and stand by Him while she "treasured all these things in her heart."[43]

It's possible that Mary of Nazareth gazed upon Him now, entering Jerusalem, still going about His Father's business. Astride His sturdy donkey, Jesus climbed toward the temple, perhaps using the monumental staircase built by Herod the Great,[44] only to come upon a disturbing sight—moneychangers in the temple.

Jesus entered the temple courts . . . *Matthew 21:12*

He went through the towering columns of the Royal Portico, the "bustling, colourful" gathering place for visiting pilgrims,[45] and promptly took action. Not only with words, but also "with force" (AMP).

. . . and drove out all who were buying and selling there. *Matthew 21:12*

Jesus "expelled" (OJB) all those doing business, allowing no time for protests or excuses. If they "bought and sold" (WYC), they were gone. Period.

He overturned the tables of the money changers and the benches of those selling doves. *Matthew 21:12*

Jesus made short work of their pop-up shops. He "turned over the four-footed tables of the money changers" (AMPC), who made a shameless profit exchanging foreign money for special coins needed to pay temple taxes. Then He pushed over the benches and chairs of those who sold "birds and animals for sacrifice" (AMP).

We seldom see His righteous anger on display, but He brought it with Him that day.

> "It is written," he said to them, "'My house will be called a house of prayer,' but you are making it 'a den of robbers.'" *Matthew 21:13*

Even at that heated moment, this Teacher's heart was showing as He invoked two passages from the prophets. First from Isaiah, "my Temple shall be called 'A House of Prayer for All People'!"[46] And then from Jeremiah, "this Temple, which bears my name, has become a den of thieves."[47] He was probably shouting by this point, so they clearly heard His opinion of their misuse of the temple—a "hideout for crooks" (CEB) and a "cave of robbers!" (LEB).

They didn't stick around for more.

Once the buyers and sellers and moneychangers scattered, "there was room for the blind and crippled to get in" (MSG).

> The blind and the lame came to him at the temple, and he healed them. *Matthew 21:14*

After the storm a measure of peace.

Jerusalem was blind, but here were people who believed in Him, asking to be blind no longer. Jerusalem contained many crooked and uneven paths, yet the pilgrims who couldn't navigate those streets trusted in Jesus, who had the power to straighten their limbs and renew their strength.

He must have stayed many hours in the temple courts healing those pressing against Him and begging to be set free from their infirmities. When we pray, we do much the same. "Please, Lord, heal me . . . fix me . . . make me well." You can be sure He cares about our physical needs today in the same way He concerned Himself with the ailments of dozens, perhaps hundreds, who asked for His touch that afternoon in Jerusalem.

Finally He required rest, as we all do. He surely returned the borrowed donkeys, as promised, and then headed east toward dinner and a bed.

> And he left them and went out of the city to Bethany,
> where he spent the night. *Matthew 21:17*

The Bible doesn't tell us where He "lodged" (ESV) in Bethany, but we can take an educated guess—in the house where three people He loved rested their heads, trusting God for tomorrow.

LAZARUS, MARY & MARTHA

Five

Ah, holy Jesus, how hast thou offended,
That we to judge thee have in hate pretended?
By foes derided, by thine own rejected,
O most afflicted!

—Translated by Robert S. Bridges,
"Ah, Holy Jesus," 1897

O Most Afflicted!

*A*cross the Judean hills dawn was breaking. Palm leaves lay discarded along the road to Jerusalem, the green fronds turning brown beneath the cloudless sky. Even at that hour Jesus and His disciples were on the move.

> Early in the morning, as Jesus was on his way back to the city, he was hungry. *Matthew 21:18*

Hard to imagine that Martha let Him slip away without breakfast. Perhaps they left so early the rest of the household hadn't stirred yet. Or maybe Jesus realized He needed something more to eat—a second breakfast, if you will. Or, true to His nature, was He taking another opportunity to teach His disciples?

I come from an entire family of teachers, so I know this to be true: teachers teach. Anytime, anywhere, on any subject. As He walked with His disciples that morning, Jesus came upon a fig tree with nothing on its branches but leaves. Hungry for its fruit, He cursed the tree, watched it wither before their eyes, and then told His followers they could perform such miracles "if you have faith and do not doubt"[1]—a reminder they would soon need.

Once they reached Jerusalem, He shared more of His wisdom while He still had a willing audience.

> Every day he was teaching at the temple. *Luke 19:47*

Monday, then Tuesday, then Wednesday, He "continued to teach" (AMPC) in the "porches and courts" (AMP), where people gathered to hear Him. He often used parables—the two sons, the ten virgins, the ten talents. Their various meanings pleased the righteous and displeased the self-righteous.

> But the chief priests, the teachers of the law and the leaders among the people were trying to kill him. *Luke 19:47*

Plain and simple, they wanted to "find a way of putting an end to him" (CJB), as the Greek makes clear. They not only wanted to destroy His body; they also wanted to destroy His reputation.

> Yet they could not find any way to do it, because all the people hung on his words. *Luke 19:48*

Within days those hangers-on would deny they knew Him. But for now the crowds were "enthralled with what they heard" (CEB). He was "a hero to the people" (TLB), who drew near, "listening to Him teach" (NLV). Like Mary of Bethany, they sat at His feet, "not wanting to miss a single word" (GNT).

Was Mary of Bethany there? Mary of Nazareth? Mary Magdalene? The Bible doesn't mention these women in the first half of what we call Holy Week but focuses on the major players in each scene. The three Marys certainly could have been present and simply were not named. For our purposes we'll picture them there, standing nearby, ready to serve.

In the same way, few of the male disciples are mentioned by name unless they have a speaking role. Jesus alone stands in the spotlight throughout the Gospels, and rightly so.

> One day as Jesus was teaching the people in the temple courts and proclaiming the good news, . . . *Luke 20:1*

In the crowded "temple complex" (HCSB), the Lord was "preaching the gospel" (ESV). Who better, since He was and forever will be the Good News? But the straightforward message Jesus was proclaiming in the temple courts that day didn't sit well with Jerusalem's leaders.

> . . . the chief priests and the teachers of the law, together with the elders, came up to him. *Luke 20:1*

They were inseparable, this group of men—the "princes of the priests" (JUB), the "experts in the law" (NET), and the "ancients" (DRA). They cut to the chase and asked Jesus a "direct question" (PHILLIPS), thrown down like a pair of gauntlets.

> "Tell us by what authority you are doing these things," they said. "Who gave you this authority?" *Luke 20:2*

First they wanted to know "What right do you have to do these things?" (CEV). And second, "Who gave you such right?" (GNT). Jesus could have revealed the whole truth, showed them

His "credentials" (MSG), told them His heavenly Father was His authority. But the hour for Him to be delivered into their hands had not yet come.

So Jesus did what rabbis do best.

> He replied, "I will also ask you a question." *Luke 20:3*

Neatly sidestepping their pointed request for information, Jesus promised to ask just "one thing" (DRA).

> ". . . John's baptism—was it from heaven, or of human origin?" *Luke 20:4*

One question and He shut them down. "They were on the spot, and knew it."[2] If they acknowledged that John's actions were ordained by God, then Jesus could claim the same. But if the religious leaders declared John's baptism a human work, the crowd would stone them to death, since the people believed "John was a prophet."[3]

What will it be, gentlemen? A rock or a hard place?

When they lamely answered, "We don't know where it was from,"[4] Jesus responded, "Then I won't tell you by what authority I do these things."[5] End of discussion.

Jesus also didn't follow their rules in the treatment of women. He was quick to include female examples in the lessons He taught—a radical move for a rabbi. One day that week He observed a woman in the temple quietly honoring God and made her the star of a short but powerful teaching.

As Jesus looked up, he saw the rich putting their gifts
into the temple treasury. *Luke 21:1*

Around the temple were thirteen trumpet-shaped containers
for offerings.[6] Some people dropped in voluntary contributions.
Others paid their annual dues to care for the temple and support
the poor. Jesus watched the wealthy "throwing their gifts into the
collection box" (CEB) as if money meant nothing to them.

He also saw a poor widow put in two very small copper
coins. *Luke 21:2*

The original Greek tells us these coppers were "fine, thin,
small, light"[7] and only "worth a penny" (CEB). My father loathed
pennies, even back in the days of penny candy. Refusing to carry
the pennies in his pocket, he gave all of them to me, which I
promptly took to the bank and turned into dollars. *Score.*

But one penny? Not much value there. Except to Jesus.

"Truly I tell you," he said, "this poor widow has put in
more than all the others." *Luke 21:3*

Her gift was far greater, not because of the amount, but because of the sacrifice required—a subject certainly on the Lord's
mind that week.

"All these people gave their gifts out of their wealth;
but she out of her poverty put in all she had to live on."
Luke 21:4

The rich gave "only what they did not need" (NCV). However large the amount, it wasn't impressive—at least not to Jesus. The destitute woman "needed that money" (ICB), and yet she gave it away to support the temple and to help the poor. Some irony there. By people's measure she had "nothing left to live on" (WE). By God's measure she had boundless faith, matchless compassion, and a heart that beat in rhythm with His.

The One who sees everything saw her gift and called it good.

But the Evil One was also paying attention that day.

> Then Satan entered Judas, called Iscariot, one of the
> Twelve. *Luke 22:3*

Satan walked right in. As if Judas left the door open by mistake. Or threw out a welcome mat on purpose. Either way "the Adversary entered" (YLT), piercing the "heart of Judas" (NLV) and prompting him to action.

> And Judas went to the chief priests and the officers of
> the temple guard and discussed with them how he
> might betray Jesus. *Luke 22:4*

Unlike Eve's conversation with a garden snake, Judas's temptation isn't recorded in Scripture. Whether it was prompted by pride, greed, or envy—three of the seven deadly sins—or pure evil at work in his soul, Judas sought out the officials and "talked about how he might hand Jesus over to them" (NLV). What hubris, thinking he wielded such power!

They were delighted and agreed to give him money.
Luke 22:5

A predictable reaction. They were "greatly pleased" (NRSV) and so "promised him a reward" (TLB). In Greek, the word translated as "money" means "silver"[8]—not copper, like the widow's two mites. No specific amount is mentioned in Luke's gospel, but Matthew tells us "thirty pieces of silver" were offered to Judas.[9]

He consented, and watched for an opportunity to
hand Jesus over to them when no crowd was present.
Luke 22:6

With that, "everything was settled" (VOICE). Having already claimed the hearts of the chief priests, teachers, and elders, now the Enemy had a mole, someone working for him on the inside. All Judas had to do was wait until "no one was around to see" (ERV). Away from the crowds. Away from the city. Away from the bright light of day.

Then came the day of Unleavened Bread on which the
Passover lamb had to be sacrificed. *Luke 22:7*

Just reading the word *sacrificed,* I feel a tightening in the pit of my stomach. The pace of events in Jerusalem was quickening.

For the next seven days, the Jewish people would eat unleavened bread, or "Thin Bread" (CEV), made without yeast, according to God's instructions before the Exodus from Egypt: "For seven days no yeast is to be found in your houses. And anyone, whether foreigner or native-born, who eats anything with yeast in it must be cut off from the community of Israel."[10]

Yeast represented sin, as if life-giving bread were "leavened with malice and wickedness."[11] Since God wanted His people to be holy, their partaking of unleavened bread was a symbol of their willingness to put aside their sin.

Then Jesus came and declared, "I am the bread of life."[12] The unleavened bread, the bread without sin, broken for us. Also for the Passover an innocent lamb "had to be killed and given on the altar in worship in the house of God,"[13] just as "Christ, our Passover lamb, has been sacrificed."[14]

There is nothing subtle about any of this. The symbolism of yeast as our sin and the lamb as our sacrifice was woven into the hearts of God's people from ancient days.

On the night of a modern Passover meal, the youngest child asks, "Why is this night different from all other nights?" That leads to an adult retelling the haggadah, the story of the Exodus—from the "suffering imposed upon the Israelites," to "the plagues visited on the Egyptians," to the "miracles performed by the Almighty for the redemption of His people."[15] From the time they were children, the men and women of Israel knew the story.

Because of Jesus, now we know the story.

Lent is a time of remembering, of revisiting the familiar scenes in Scripture and discovering what God wants us to learn this year. We are not the same women we were twelve months ago. Our lives have changed, and our perspectives have shifted. Even so, "Jesus Christ is the same yesterday and today and forever."[16] His love for us has not changed, and our need for Him has not diminished.

Let's press on, my sister, aware of the agony that is to come and the triumph that will follow.

> Jesus sent Peter and John, saying, "Go and make prepa-
> rations for us to eat the Passover." *Luke 22:8*

His go-to guys, Peter and John, were sent ahead to "prepare
our *Seder*" (CJB). The traditional meal involved "meat roasted over
the fire, along with bitter herbs, and bread made without yeast,"[17]
requiring the disciples to make a trip to the market stalls en route.
They no doubt paid inflated festival prices for their goods. Surely
that was a common thing even two thousand years ago. And they
needed a quiet place to meet.

> "Where do you want us to prepare for it?" they asked.
> *Luke 22:9*

It's the biggest event on the Jewish calendar, and they were asking this now? Apparently that was standard operating procedure
when traveling with Jesus. Everything was on a need-to-know basis.
Part of trusting God is letting go of our need to know and refusing to fret over the who, what, when, where, and why. When the
time comes, the Lord will inform us, just as He did His disciples.

> He replied, "As you enter the city, a man carrying a jar
> of water will meet you. Follow him to the house that he
> enters, . . ." *Luke 22:10*

Sounds a bit mysterious. "Keep your eyes open as you enter
the city" (MSG), Jesus told them. "There shall meet you a man,
bearing a pitcher of water" (YLT). Since women carried jars and
men used leather skins for water,[18] this stranger would be easily
spotted on the crowded Jerusalem streets.

Why the clandestine approach? Jesus wanted them to dine in a safe place, where His enemies wouldn't find them. He required only the company of His disciples that evening—just the Twelve. More instructions for Peter and John.

> "... and say to the owner of the house, 'The Teacher asks: Where is the guest room, where I may eat the Passover with my disciples?'" *Luke 22:11*

The homeowner was no doubt a trustworthy follower of Christ who would make them welcome and not tell a soul about the men meeting in his "guest-chamber" (ASV) to "eat the pasch" (DRA).

> "He will show you a large room upstairs, all furnished. Make preparations there." *Luke 22:12*

A "great high chamber" (GNV) indicates the owner was a man of means, who could offer a "spacious second-story room, swept and ready" (MSG). The roof would have been flat with an outside stairway for access.[19] As for being "furnished," the Greek simply means "spread,"[20] like the cloaks spread across the road on Palm Sunday.[21] Rather than envisioning a massive dining table with wooden chairs, picture several low couches around a table.

> They left and found things just as Jesus had told them. So they prepared the Passover. *Luke 22:13*

Such obedience. Jesus told them what to do, and they did it. They didn't complain, ask a dozen questions, or whine about having to make dinner.

In accord with the Passover tradition, the two disciples took a lamb without blemish to the temple that afternoon to be sacrificed and butchered. Then they roasted the meat in oil or wine[22] in one of the many outdoor clay ovens built each year for the festival.[23] Bearing the savory meat, the men returned to the upper room where the others were waiting for them.

Sunset marked the end of one day and the start of another. Perhaps the women were gathering for the Passover meal in nearby Bethany, while in this room thirteen men met for their last supper together.

> When evening came, Jesus was reclining at the table with the Twelve. *Matthew 26:20*

Put aside any thoughts of Leonardo da Vinci's famous painting *The Last Supper,* in which Jesus and the disciples are seated in chairs on one side of a long, elegant table with tapestries on the walls behind them and a pastoral view out the window. The artist's conception is more fifteenth century than first century.

At the real supper in Jerusalem, the men reclined to eat—"the posture for a banquet"[24] —just as they had in Bethany when Martha served and Mary anointed. The guest list was short with no visitors, as Jesus intended.

> Jesus knew that the Father had put all things under his power, and that he had come from God and was returning to God; . . . *John 13:3*

We feel the scene beginning to shift. The room and the meal were no longer the focus. A different kind of preparation was taking place. Jesus knew this would be His "last night on earth."[25]

> . . . so he got up from the meal, . . . *John 13:4*

Jesus didn't merely stand. He "riseth" (KJV)—the same Greek word used to describe His resurrection.[26] As He stood, it was as if His departure from this world had already begun.

> . . . took off his outer clothing, and wrapped a towel
> around his waist. *John 13:4*

The disciples knew nothing of what was to come. Jesus knew everything. The outer garments He'd just cast aside would soon be taken from Him. For now He removed them willingly and assumed the role of a servant.

> After that, he poured water into a basin and
> began to wash his disciples' feet, drying them
> with the towel that was wrapped around him.
> *John 13:5*

Oh, Lord Jesus.

We were undone watching Mary of Bethany bathe His feet. But this. The humility, the humanity, the sheer grittiness of an act considered so demeaning it was reserved for Gentile slaves.[27] Surely the room was filled with a holy silence as pure and sweet as Mary's perfume.

Jesus moved from one man to the next, inching the basin

along the floor. If He spoke, His words were not recorded. Only His actions. Washing and then drying.

> He came to Simon Peter, who said to him, "Lord, are you going to wash my feet?" *John 13:6*

Of course Peter had something to say. When Jesus once asked the Twelve, "Who do the crowds say I am?"[28] Peter was the one who answered, "God's Messiah."[29] He was born to be bold, to speak his mind, to proclaim the truth.

> Jesus replied, "You do not realize now what I am doing, but later you will understand." *John 13:7*

A tender response. Jesus didn't want to burden Peter or the others with more knowledge than they could handle.

> "No," said Peter, "you shall never wash my feet." *John 13:8*

Did Peter shrink back from Jesus's touch in the same way you and I sometimes refuse to accept His forgiveness—because we believe we're not worthy of it?

> Jesus answered, "Unless I wash you, you have no part with me." *John 13:8*

Earlier that day Jesus had preached the gospel. Here He demonstrated it. Our fellowship with Him depends on our being made clean, made righteous. We cannot bathe ourselves spiritually. He alone can wash away our sins. Otherwise, He says, "You don't really belong to me" (CEV).

> "Then, Lord," Simon Peter replied, "not just my feet but my hands and my head as well!" *John 13:9*

Peter was not one for half measures. He was all in. "Wash my hands! Wash my head!" (MSG).

> Jesus answered, "Those who have had a bath need only to wash their feet; their whole body is clean." *John 13:10*

This isn't water-and-soap clean Jesus is talking about. It's righteousness clean. It's His forgiveness, His grace that washes His people from head to toe. "My concern, you understand, is holiness, not hygiene" (MSG).

> "And you are clean, though not every one of you."
> *John 13:10*

Having spoken those cryptic words, Jesus stood and pulled on His discarded garment and then joined his disciples at the table. He apparently didn't name Judas or glance his direction, so every man present must have wondered whom He meant. Then during the meal He made a second reference to the person among them who was untrustworthy.

> And while they were eating, he said, "Truly I tell you, one of you will betray me." *Matthew 26:21*

This time the disciples understood. When Jesus used a word like *betray*, He meant it.

> They were very sad and began to say to him one
> after the other, "Surely you don't mean me, Lord?"
> *Matthew 26:22*

In his famous mural, da Vinci captured in tempera paint the disciples' consternation. The Word tells us they were "greatly distressed" (NLT), "terribly upset" (CJB), and "deeply grieved" (AMP). Though Jesus said only one would betray Him, each man may have feared the Lord meant him. Perhaps that was the Lord's intent. That all of them—and each one of us—would ask, "Am I the one?" (TLB).

> Jesus replied, "The one who has dipped his hand
> into the bowl with me will betray me." *Matthew
> 26:23*

Food was served in communal dishes. A practical method, if not very sanitary. Judas must have been reclining quite near Jesus to have reached in at the same time.

> "The Son of Man will go just as it is written about
> him. But woe to that man who betrays the Son of
> Man! It would be better for him if he had not been
> born." *Matthew 26:24*

A prophecy fulfilled, yes, but that didn't let Judas off the hook. His actions were still evil. He was still doomed.

> Then Judas, the one who would betray him, said,
> "Surely you don't mean me, Rabbi?" *Matthew 26:25*

Was Judas testing the waters here? Or taunting Him? Perhaps he was trying to deflect the rest from suspecting him. Judas repeated what the others had said, with one exception. They called Him "Lord." Judas called Him "Teacher." There were many rabbis in Jerusalem. But only one Lord of all.

When Judas said, "I am not the one. Am I?" (ICB), Jesus put the responsibility of answering the question right where it belonged—on him.

> "You have said so." *Matthew 26:25*

Something about this story gnaws at my conscience. Could I ever betray Jesus? Take a job where His name is defiled and derided and then join in the chorus because I need the money? Marry a man with wealth but no faith and follow in his footsteps rather than following Christ?

In all of history there is only one Judas. But his unique betrayal of Jesus stands as a stark reminder of how base our human nature can be. "The heart is deceitful above all things and beyond cure. Who can understand it?"[30] We know the answer: only One can plumb the deepest places no human can see. "I the LORD search the heart and examine the mind."[31]

Jesus knew the heart and mind of everyone in the upper room that night in Jerusalem. Having drawn out His betrayer, He was ready to affirm the faith of those who remained loyal to Him. As the meal drew to a close, He reached for the unleavened bread and a cup of wine, introducing a ritual that was not part of the

Passover but something entirely new. "Take and eat; this is my body,"[32] He said. Then "drink from it, all of you."[33] And so a beautiful sacrament was born: the Eucharist, Communion, the Lord's Supper.

> When they had sung a hymn, . . . *Matthew 26:30*

A perfect way to end their time together, "singing songs of praise" (CEB), likely portions of Psalms 113–118, known as the Hallel, traditionally sung during the Passover meal.[34] The men often sang antiphonally, meaning Jesus sang each line first, and then the disciples responded, "Hallelujah!"[35]

Even facing death, Jesus praised His Father in song.

When the last note had faded into silence, Jesus and His disciples slipped down the outer stair.

> . . . they went out to the Mount of Olives. *Matthew 26:30*

After a short walk through the Kidron Valley—no more than thirty minutes once they exited the city gates—they reached their destination. Was it a dark night, or were the hills bathed in moonlight? Did a warm breeze rustle the olive trees, or was the air still? We know only what was said, and it was bleak news indeed.

> Then Jesus told them, "This very night you will all fall away on account of me, . . ." *Matthew 26:31*

Only Judas would betray Him, but all would be "ashamed" (NLV) or "offended" (ASV) or "disillusioned" (AMP) or "scandalized"

(DRA) because of Him. Friend, those are four very different things! That suggests the original Greek is hard to translate into English. Literally, it means putting a snare in the way and causing someone to stumble.[36] Jesus was accepting responsibility for the confusion about to ensue. "This very night all of you will run away and leave me" (GNT), He explained, offering them freedom from their guilt, placing the weight on His own shoulders.

The prophet Zechariah had forewarned of this night—again, five hundred years before it happened.

> ". . . for it is written:
>
> "'I will strike the shepherd,
>   and the sheep of the flock will be scattered.'"
>   *Matthew 26:31*

Who is the *I,* the One doing the striking? His heavenly Father, the Lord Almighty. "Awake, sword, against my shepherd, against the man who is close to me!"[37] When we stand with the women at the foot of the cross, we'll recall these words with fear and trembling: "I will strike the shepherd dead" (CJB).

This is how much God the Father loves us: He was "pleased to crush Him, putting Him to grief"[38] so we might live and no longer be scattered "in all directions" (CEB), lost in the wilderness. If you've ever been lost—spiritually, physically, emotionally, relationally—separated from home, from safety, from a meaningful life, from people who care about you, Jesus came so you could be found, and He died so you could be set free from your sin.

No wonder we call Him our Savior!

Now watch how Jesus redirected their thoughts.

"But after I have risen, . . ." *Matthew 26:32*

Oh, what hope! In the face of imminent betrayal, abandonment, torture, and death, Jesus said without hesitation, "After I have been raised from the dead . . ." (NLT). There was no doubt in His mind, and there must be no doubt in ours, beloved. He died willingly at the hands of men, and He rose triumphantly at the hands of God.

That night in Jerusalem He was preparing His disciples for the separation to come and informing them where their paths would next cross.

". . . I will go ahead of you into Galilee." *Matthew 26:32*

Imagine how they felt at hearing their Teacher was to be struck down, raised from the dead, and then transported north to Galilee, where He would "meet" (NLT) them! Their emotions had to be reeling, especially in view of the prophecy about their deserting Him.

Peter replied, "Even if all fall away on account of you, I never will." *Matthew 26:33*

Peter, the rock on which Christ would build His church,[39] said what all of us might say at a moment like this, wanting to sound brave, hoping to encourage Him. "All the other followers may lose their faith in you. But my faith will never be shaken" (ERV).

The Lord knew better and set Peter straight.

> "Truly I tell you," Jesus answered, "this very night, be-
> fore the rooster crows, you will disown me three times."
> *Matthew 26:34*

Jesus wasn't suggesting it *might* happen. He was informing
Peter, "You will say three times that you do not know me" (we).
He didn't mean Peter would deny His existence. Rather, he would
deny their friendship. This is what matters to the Lord—our relationship with Him.

No doubt deeply hurt, Peter refused to accept the truth.

> But Peter declared, "Even if I have to die with you, I will
> never disown you." And all the other disciples said the
> same. *Matthew 26:35*

Peter wanted to believe that he would be faithful to the end.
The rest of them wanted to believe it too. So do you and I and all
who claim to know Him.

But then I remember a conversation I had with a businessman
at the start of a long cross-country flight. After he regaled me with
all his successes, punctuating his speech with vulgarities, he asked,
"So what do you do?"

"I'm a writer," I told him, hoping that would put an end to it.
I was pretty sure this guy didn't want to hear about Jesus and even
more sure I didn't want to broach the topic and risk a scathing
attack.

"Oh yeah?" was his comeback. "What do you write?"

"Books for women," I answered, certain *that* would shut him
down.

"Really? What are they about?"

What are they about, Liz? "Faith," I blurted out and then reached for the in-flight magazine, utterly ashamed of myself.

My responses were true. But all of them denied Jesus. Skirted around His name. Avoided His gospel truth. Because I was afraid the man might—what? Roll his eyes? Throw his drink in my face?

God forgave me, because He is good. And He has bolstered my courage, because He will not be denied. Now when a stranger asks what I do, I joyfully respond, "I love Jesus, and so I write books about Him." It's a conversation starter for sure.

What we *think* we'll do when our faith is put to the test and what we *actually* do are often two different things, as Jesus's men were about to discover.

> Then Jesus went with his disciples to a place called Gethsemane, . . . *Matthew 26:36*

An olive orchard near the foot of the Mount of Olives,[40] Gethsemane was a quiet place, away from the clamor of the city. It was late now, nearing midnight.[41] The men were exhausted as they found places to sit among the gnarled trunks of the olive trees, many of them hundreds of years old.

> . . . and he said to them, "Sit here while I go over there and pray." *Matthew 26:36*

How far was "over there"? Luke tells us, "He withdrew about a stone's throw beyond them."[42] Enough distance to find some privacy with His Father, yet close enough for Him to point out, "I shall pray yonder" (YLT).

But Jesus did not go alone.

> He took Peter and the two sons of Zebedee along with
> him, . . . *Matthew 26:37*

He chose Peter, who'd promised to stick by Him, plus "the two brothers, James and John" (CEV), and together they moved to a separate spot.

> . . . and he began to be sorrowful and troubled.
> *Matthew 26:37*

In the silence, in the darkness, the reality of what was about to happen must have crushed Him as thoroughly as olives in a press, leaving the Son of Man "grieved and greatly distressed" (AMP). The fullness of His humanity weighs on our hearts as we watch Him suffer emotionally, knowing He will soon suffer physically beyond anything we could ever bear or imagine.

The Lord confessed the depth of His pain to Peter, James, and John.

> Then he said to them, "My soul is overwhelmed with
> sorrow to the point of death." *Matthew 26:38*

We can hear the anguish in His voice, feel the agony in His words. "My heart is so heavy with grief, I feel as if I am dying" (ERV). We all have faced hard things, have lived through seasons of grief and suffering, but we haven't looked at our hands and known that nails would pierce them in a matter of hours and that life would drain from our bodies while strangers mocked us and spat on us.

Lord Jesus, we cannot fathom such love.

Having admitted His sorrow, He asked for help.

> "Stay here and keep watch with me." *Matthew 26:38*

Keeping watch meant staying awake and alert. Not an easy thing for His men to do after a busy day in the temple courts and then a long evening over wine and meat. Jesus moved away from them, perhaps not wanting them to hear what He was about to say.

> Going a little farther, he fell with his face to the ground and prayed, "My Father, if it is possible, may this cup be taken from me." *Matthew 26:39*

Our hearts are pierced. No wonder He asked for this reprieve. Who wouldn't? The cup was not only suffering and death; it was also God's wrath.[43] Jesus is no less our hero for not wanting to drink from so terrible a cup.

But He didn't pause for an answer, didn't wait for a reprieve. He kept praying.

> "Yet . . ." *Matthew 26:39*

You're stopping after one word, Liz? I am.

Yet is the whole of the Christian life. "Nevertheless" (ESV), we do God's will. "However" (CEB), despite wishing to do things our way, we do them His way. "Even so" (NLV), His plan is the plan, and it is good.

What Jesus said that night is what we must say every day of our lives.

> ". . . not as I will, but as you will." *Matthew 26:39*

We are all strong willed. Even the meek and mild and malleable among us prefer to do as we choose. To be Christlike is to live with these words on our lips: "Not what I desire, but what you desire" (WEB). Bending to His will can be a lifelong battle. Or it can be one heartrending instance of complete surrender, followed by a lifetime of acknowledging and resting in His sovereignty and grace.

Jesus has shown us how to embrace God's plan, and He will, without question, give us the strength to do it.

In any story—in any history—there comes a pivotal moment, often called the point of no return in a storytelling framework. A decision is made, a vow is spoken, and then things quickly go downhill, careening out of control, headed for certain disaster. Jesus found His disciples—the three He'd asked to stay awake— asleep on their watch and said to them, "The spirit is willing, but the flesh is weak."[44] Yes, it is, Lord, and we know it well.

After praying in solitude three times, then returning from each entreaty to find His disciples asleep, Jesus announced the hour had come for Him to be delivered into the hands of sinners. He called out, "Rise! Let us go! Here comes my betrayer!"[45]

And there was Judas. He arrived with a "large crowd armed with swords and clubs."[46] Judas said, " 'Greetings, Rabbi!' and kissed him."[47] Even then, Jesus called him "friend,"[48] meaning a cousin, a clansman, a companion,[49] not a common thief.

When Jesus was seized and arrested, He told the priests, officers, and elders who had come for him, "This is your hour—when darkness reigns."[50] Exactly as He'd predicted, "all the disciples deserted him and fled,"[51] seeking the cover of night.

Jesus not only accepted this reality, but He also was prepared for it, knowing that in the dreaded hours to come, He would not be alone. *The women would be there.*

It's heartening to realize that Scripture has no parallel stories of women betraying Jesus, denying Jesus, or abandoning Jesus. "They are not like the disciple-defectors."[52] His female followers were loyal to Him from start to finish. In the hours to come, we'll watch them prove their devotion, even in the most desperate circumstances.

Six

O sacred Head, now wounded, with
   grief and shame weighed down,
Now scornfully surrounded with **thorns,
   thine only crown:**
How pale thou art with anguish, with sore
   abuse and scorn!
How does that visage languish which once
   was bright as morn!

—Translated by James W. Alexander,
"O Sacred Head, Now Wounded," 1830

Thorns Thine
Only Crown

*D*arkness was all around her.

Mary of Nazareth stood, abandoning her borrowed bed. Though it was past midnight, she had no hope of sleeping. Her son had been betrayed by a friend and then arrested by strangers. How was that possible?

Days earlier she'd come from Nazareth for the Passover, a nameless fear thudding in her heart. Simeon's prophecy, seldom far from her thoughts, now consumed her. "This child is destined . . . to be a sign that will be spoken against."[1] Finally she understood. Jesus was loved, even revered, in Galilee, but here in Jerusalem her son was hated and reviled.

Mary quietly moved toward the window, careful not to wake the others sleeping on pallets scattered around the small room. When she looked down on the empty courtyard, all was silent. Simeon's words pressed in, sharper than ever. "And a sword will pierce your own soul too."[2]

The burden of that prediction, spoken just forty days after she gave birth to her firstborn, had grown heavier with each passing year. "A sword will wound your own soul" (NIrV), the prophet Simeon had told her as they'd stood in the temple courts, Joseph by her side. "Yes, a long knife will cut your heart" (WE).

She'd first sensed the sharp edge of that blade after the Passover when they were separated from their young son for three long days. Then, not so long ago, another glancing blow to her heart occurred in the unlikeliest of places.

> A wedding took place at Cana in Galilee. Jesus' mother was there, and Jesus and his disciples had also been invited to the wedding. *John 2:1–2*

It's a special blessing whenever my son, Matt, sits beside me in public. Surely Mary felt the same way. Proud. Loved. Appreciated. Grateful. The Lord's growing number of followers were "bidden" (ASV) to join the party as well. We can picture this small but lively group seated on benches beneath a cloudless sky, wine cups in hand, enjoying the festivities.

> When the wine was gone, Jesus' mother said to him, "They have no more wine." *John 2:3*

Mary probably felt sorry for the host, who stood "on the brink of embarrassment" (VOICE). Running out of wine was a social disaster, especially at a wedding. So "Jesus' mother came to him with the problem" (TLB).

> "Woman, why do you involve me?" Jesus replied.
> *John 2:4*

His response may sound critical to our ears, but the word *woman* was "a respectful form of address in that culture."[3] Though Mary hadn't asked Him to do anything about the wine, Jesus knew her heart, knew her intent, which is why He asked her, "Dear woman, why are you telling me about this?" (NIrV).

Before Mary had a chance to reply, He voiced His concern.

"My hour has not yet come." *John 2:4*

In the original Greek it's literally "the hour of me."[4] Whatever His tone, Mary must have felt chastened. Now that He'd begun to gather a following, she may have thought her son was ready "to act and to be revealed" (AMP). Not so, it seemed. He told her plainly, "The time for me to show who I really am isn't here yet" (NIrV).

Still wanting to provide wine for the wedding party, Mary played the mother card. She put the problem in her son's hands yet made her wishes clear by setting things in motion.

His mother said to the servants, "Do whatever he tells you." *John 2:5*

Was she defying His wishes or following His Father's leading? We can be certain only of what happened. "She went ahead anyway" (MSG) and told the household servants, "Whatever He says to you, do it" (NASB).

Jesus said to the servants, "Fill the jars with water"; so they filled them to the brim. *John 2:7*

No questions asked, they filled the jars "up to the very top" (NET). We can picture these obedient servants barely containing their excitement as they watched clear water change into wine before their eyes. How like Jesus to ensure the least of these were the first to see His miracle.

When the master of the banquet tasted the wine and commented on its exceptional quality, no one in the household pointed to Jesus. But Mary knew what had happened. So did His disciples.

> What Jesus did here in Cana of Galilee was the first of
> the signs through which he revealed his glory; and his
> disciples believed in him. *John 2:11*

His "wonderworks" (AMPC) began that day when He "demonstrated his power" (PHILLIPS) and "showed his divine greatness" (ERV). The motivation for His miracles was always the same—He wanted people to believe in Him, trust in Him, put their faith in Him. That day in Cana, Jesus chose to do His mother's will and, even more, to honor His Father's will, revealing His true identity to those closest to Him.

Mary, too, showed us something about herself. She'd become a mature, self-assured woman over the years. No longer a young virgin, meek and mild, she had a faith honed by experience and expectation. She believed the prophecies about her son and believed in His calling. So, like any mother in any century, she encouraged Him to use His gifts.

Even so, she must have felt Him draw a step further away from her that day in Cana, realizing the time of her authority was over.[5] In the same way a grown son will "leave his father and mother and be united to his wife,"[6] Jesus was leaving His mother and preparing to unite with His bride, the church.[7]

His earthly father, Joseph, is not mentioned in the scene at Cana. Most scholars believe he was deceased before the year of Jesus's passion, leaving Mary a widow.[8]

Now, years later, we find her in Jerusalem watching her son face His accusers. The grim hours ahead would test every ounce of her courage, even as the sword Simeon had warned her about had begun to pierce her "innermost being."[9]

> The chief priests and the whole Sanhedrin were looking for evidence against Jesus so that they could put him to death, . . . *Mark 14:55*

Such vile hatred toward the One we love is unfathomable. The fact that these were religious men makes it even more bewildering. But Jesus understood them well, having once told the Pharisees, "You belong to your father, the devil, and you want to carry out your father's desires. He was a murderer from the beginning, not holding to the truth, for there is no truth in him. When he lies, he speaks his native language, for he is a liar and the father of lies. Yet because I tell the truth, you do not believe me!"[10]

Is it any wonder "the whole Jewish council tried to find something that Jesus had done wrong so they could kill him" (NCV)? All they needed was a valid reason, some solid evidence, a credible testimony.

> . . . but they did not find any. *Mark 14:55*

Even Jesus's enemies discovered nothing bad about Him, and you know they tried their best. Still, "the council could find no proof against him" (ICB).

> Many testified falsely against him, but their statements did not agree. *Mark 14:56*

They couldn't get their fabricated stories straight and so "contradicted each other" (CEB) and broke one of the Ten Commandments they claimed to cherish: "You shall not give false testimony against your neighbor."[11]

> "We heard him say, 'I will destroy this temple made with human hands and in three days will build another, not made with hands.'" *Mark 14:58*

Wait. The Lord didn't say *He* would tear down the temple. He said *they* would. "Destroy this temple, and I will raise it again in three days."[12] A lie is the truth turned upside down, and these sons of Satan were proficient at standing on their heads.

> Yet even then their testimony did not agree. *Mark 14:59*

Perhaps to put an end to their fumbling, Caiaphas, the high priest and self-appointed enemy of Jesus, turned to Him and demanded He answer their charges.

> But Jesus remained silent and gave no answer. *Mark 14:61*

The One who is Peace itself held His peace. But when Caiaphas asked Jesus if He was the Messiah, He could not keep silent.

> "I am," said Jesus. *Mark 14:62*

His words struck like a lightning bolt. " 'I AM,' answered Yeshua" (cjb). Think of all the times in His Word that the Lord affirms who He is: "I am the bread of life,"[13] "I am the light of the world,"[14] and "I am the good shepherd."[15] The Greek word *eimi* means "I am, I exist," and the word before it, *ego,* is an emphatic *"I."*[16] Imagine Him saying, *"I* . . . I am!"

> "And you will see the Son of Man sitting at the right hand of the Mighty One and coming on the clouds of heaven." *Mark 14:62*

At that, Caiaphas was undone.

> The high priest tore his clothes. "Why do we need any more witnesses?" he asked. *Mark 14:63*

He "ripped his robe apart" (cev)—a dramatic way of expressing his "horror" (nlt), "outrage" (exb), and "indignation" (amp)—and then asked the crowd for their verdict.

> They all condemned him as worthy of death. *Mark 14:64*

Because these men did not understand that Jesus was the Son of God, they considered His claims blasphemous and agreed He "must be killed" (ERV).

We have no proof that the women who supported Him were present at that dark hour, but His Word takes us all there. We can't look away, beloved, and we can't wish it away. This is the historical record of what Jesus did for us—and what He asks of us. He said, "Whoever wants to be my disciple must deny themselves and take up their cross daily and follow me."[17]

In this agonizing scene He shows us what that means.

> Then some began to spit at him; . . . *Mark 14:65*

These religious men were spitting like beasts of burden, their saliva stinging His skin, their actions demeaning His humanity. The Lord had prepared His followers earlier, telling them that people would "mock him, insult him and spit on him."[18] Though He knew this was coming, in no way would that make it easier to bear.

> . . . they blindfolded him, struck him with their fists, and said, "Prophesy!" *Mark 14:65*

They "covered his face" (CEB) so He couldn't see them, and then they demanded, "Prove that you are a prophet!" (ICB) and "Tell us who hit you!" (CEV). Even as they shouted, they continued "pounding him with their fists" (CJB).

His punishment had only begun. It seemed everyone wanted to do Him harm.

> And the guards took him and beat him. *Mark 14:65*

It's not clear who these men were—"officers" (ASV) or "temple police" (HCSB) or "servants" (DRA), which is closest to the Greek meaning. What's certain is they "slapped him as they took him away" (NLT) and kept "striking him with their palms" (YLT). The Greek word is very specific here, meaning "a blow with the palm of the hand."[19]

Mary of Bethany had *anointed* Him with her palms.

The crowd had *adored* Him with their palms.

Now guards *abused* Him with their palms.

Enough, enough! rings through our hearts. But the day was far from over, and the worst was yet to come. During Lent it's tempting to hurry toward Easter morning, eager to declare, "He is risen!" Yes, He certainly is. But reminding ourselves what came before His glorious victory over death is how we remain humbled by His sacrifice and grateful for His mercy.

We were "bought at a price."[20] This was the cost.

> And they said many other insulting things to him. *Luke 22:65*

Here is some consolation: these "evil and slanderous" (AMPC) words they spoke, the "horrible things" (CEB) they shouted at Him, weren't recorded. But any family, any friends who were there to support Him must have winced at every blow and cringed at every word.

Elsewhere that black night one of the Lord's most trusted companions struck far deeper blows—not with his palms but with his words.

Jesus had told Peter, "Before the rooster crows, you will disown me three times."[21] Peter did exactly that, denying his relationship with Christ when approached by a servant girl in the courtyard[22] and then by a woman in the gateway.[23] When several people questioned him, noticing his Galilean accent, Peter "began to call down curses, and he swore to them, 'I don't know the man!'"[24]

Then a rooster crowed.

Peter "went outside and wept bitterly."[25] Of the more than two dozen prophecies fulfilled that day, this one is especially memorable. We grieve with Peter because we see ourselves in this disciple—loyal to Christ when it's convenient but not when it might cost us something.

Forgive us, Lord, as You forgave Peter. Strengthen us when our times of testing come.

Around six o'clock a faint wash of gold appeared in the eastern sky before sunlight spilled over the horizon and into the streets of Jerusalem.

At daybreak . . . *Luke 22:66*

When "morning came" (CEB), things grew worse for Jesus. He spent the early hours being dragged from one authority to another by the usual suspects—"the chief priests and the teachers of the law."[26] We know the disciples fled, but we can't be certain who remained. We know only that a "whole assembly"[27] of people led Jesus off to see Pontius Pilate, the Roman governor of Judea.

To their dismay Pilate told the crowd, "I find no basis for a charge against this man"[28] and then sent the Lord to Herod Antipas, the reigning tetrarch of Galilee, "who was also in Jerusalem at that time."[29] Herod was glad to see Jesus, hoping He might perform a sign of some sort. But Jesus wasn't there to impress Herod with miracles or to answer his questions. So Herod and his soldiers ridiculed and mocked Jesus and then sent Him back to Pilate.[30]

Pilate was probably not at all pleased to see Jesus a second time. "He has done nothing to deserve death,"[31] Pilate insisted. "Therefore, I will punish him and then release him."[32]

Yes, we plead, even now. *Please release Him.* We're undone at the thought of our beloved Savior being nailed to a cross. But just as Christ was willing to die, we must be willing to embrace the truth of His crucifixion, knowing it was entirely for our benefit.

The crowd didn't want Jesus punished. They wanted Him killed. "Away with this man! Release Barabbas to us!"[33] they shouted. Barabbas had been imprisoned for murder and insurrection,[34] yet they considered Jesus the greater threat to society.

Only one gospel account includes this next vital detail:

> While Pilate was sitting on the judge's seat, his wife sent him this message: . . . *Matthew 27:19*

Later sources identify her as Claudia, but the Bible tells us only her marital status—the wife of Pilate. Still, we can sort out a few things. She had sufficient courage and confidence to interrupt her husband on "the judge's bench" (HCSB) while he was "presiding over the court" (TLB). She also wasn't hesitant to speak her mind or make a bold request.

We're not told how she sent word to her husband. Did she dispatch a servant? Carve the words on a clay tablet? Seek him out in person? Over the centuries some artists have shown her standing behind her husband, whispering in his ear. All these scenarios have storytelling appeal, but we can be certain only of her message, recorded in Scripture.

> . . . "Don't have anything to do with that innocent
> man, . . ." *Matthew 27:19*

Strong words, sister! "Have nothing to do with that good
Man" (NLV), she told her husband. "Leave that righteous man
alone" (CEB). How did she know Jesus was "just and upright"
(AMPC)? The rumors around Jerusalem would have been mixed.
But in her sleep God had revealed the truth.

> ". . . for I have suffered a great deal today in a dream be-
> cause of him." *Matthew 27:19*

Awakened by terrible "nightmares" (CEV) that were "full of
twisted sufferings" (VOICE), she felt compelled to inform her husband of Jesus's innocence.

Either Pilate loved his wife or trusted in the power of dreams,
because he acted on her counsel immediately.

> Wanting to release Jesus, Pilate appealed to them again.
> *Luke 23:20*

However loudly he "called out to them" (NKJV), however much
he longed to "set Jesus free" (CEV), the crowd would have none of it.

> But they kept shouting, "Crucify him! Crucify him!"
> *Luke 23:21*

What had He done to anger them so? Pilate seemed at a loss
to explain it and was loath to accept it.

For the third time he spoke to them: . . . *Luke 23:22*

Three denials by Peter. Three appeals by Pilate. The number three echoes through the Passion, as it does throughout the Bible.[35] The Trinity is Father, Son, and Holy Spirit. Creation is time, space, and matter. People are body, soul, and spirit. Here, *the third time* tells us this will be Pilate's last effort on the Lord's behalf.

> . . . "Why? What crime has this man committed? I have found in him no grounds for the death penalty. Therefore I will have him punished and then release him." *Luke 23:22*

Pilate's efforts to appease his anxious wife and spare an innocent man were in vain. Blinded by hate rather than bound by the law, the angry crowd made their wishes clear.

> But with loud shouts they insistently demanded that he be crucified, and their shouts prevailed. *Luke 23:23*

Wanting to experience this scene in full, I tried shouting "Crucify him!" in my writing study and couldn't get above a whisper. Not because someone might have heard me, but because the terrible words made me sick to my stomach.

Yet this feverish crowd in Jerusalem was "unrelenting" (AMP) in their demands. "Crucify him! Crucify him!" Their voices "waxed strong" (WYC) and so in the end "won out" (CEB).

> Wanting to satisfy the crowd, Pilate released Barabbas to them. *Mark 15:15*

Pontius Pilate was the worst kind of people pleaser. "Afraid of a riot" (TLB) and "desiring to placate the crowd" (OJB), he set Barabbas free and showed no mercy to Jesus, the giver of mercy.

> He had Jesus flogged, and handed him over to be crucified. *Mark 15:15*

Pilate "ordered his soldiers to beat Jesus" (CEV) using a "lead-tipped whip" (NLT). Several short whips, actually, fashioned with tiny lead balls and sharpened sheep bones. The whips tore at His skin and inflicted unimaginable pain. Though flogging was "the normal prelude to crucifixion" (VOICE), there is nothing normal about such an inhumane act.

Could you bear to watch? Could any of us?

The Jewish leaders and Roman soldiers were not done with Him, so great was their appetite for inflicting pain. If the women who loved Him were present, we can be sure they clung to one another, praying for God the Father to comfort His suffering Son.

Jesus did not resist arrest, did not run away, did not refuse to be mocked. Instead, "Christ loved us and gave himself up for us as a fragrant offering and sacrifice to God."[36] What we call senseless violence He called a sweet aroma. What we call punishment He called sacrifice.

I will spare you what I can, but these are the most important scenes in the Bible, spread across all four gospels. We are meant to read them. And we are meant to be overwhelmed, if only by His love for us.

> The soldiers led Jesus away into the palace (that is, the
> Praetorium) and called together the whole company of
> soldiers. *Mark 15:16*

They dragged Him "inside the courtyard of the fortress" (CEV), the palace in Jerusalem occupied by the Roman governor. There they assembled the entire company, about five hundred soldiers.[37]

> They put a purple robe on him, then twisted together a
> crown of thorns and set it on him. *Mark 15:17*

His purple robe—the color of royalty—was a mockery of this King of the Jews. Then they braided "a big ring of thorns" (WE) into a makeshift crown. Although there is a plant today called the crown of thorns, the flexible qundaul, with its sharp, one-inch spikes, is more likely what they had on hand.

Think of this: when the Roman soldiers pressed the crown of thorns onto His head, "Mary's fragrant spikenard was still in His hair."[38] Mary of Bethany's sacrificial gift was with Him even then, anointing Him still.

> Again and again they struck him on the head with a
> staff and spit on him. *Mark 15:19*

It went on and on "for a long while" (VOICE), as hundreds of soldiers shouted, and those who were closest "kept beating His head with a reed" (NASB). They sought to pummel His pride, not understanding He'd laid it aside at birth, when He gave up heaven and came to earth.

> Falling on their knees, they paid homage to him. *Mark 15:19*

The soldiers "pretended to honor him" (NIrV) and did just the opposite, bowing their knees "in mock worship" (CJB) "as if to give him great respect" (WE). Physical pain, mental anguish, emotional trauma—these men withheld nothing.

All the while His heavenly Father watched. "For God so loved the world that he gave his one and only Son."[39] Mary of Nazareth gave her son too. The crown of thorns pressed into her son's brow surely pierced her heart as deeply as any sword.

> And when they had mocked him, they took off the purple robe and put his own clothes on him. Then they led him out to crucify him. *Mark 15:20*

A tried and tested Roman method of execution, crucifixion required the condemned to be "nailed to a cross" (NLV) somewhere beyond the city walls on a busy thoroughfare, where all could see the power of Rome on public display.

The hour was nearing nine o'clock in the morning.

> As the soldiers led him away, they seized Simon from Cyrene, who was on his way in from the country, and put the cross on him and made him carry it behind Jesus. *Luke 23:26*

Only John's gospel mentions Jesus "carrying his own cross."[40] Perhaps He struggled beneath the weight of it, such that the soldiers "grabbed hold of a man" (CJB) named Simon, a native of

Cyrene—modern Libya—and forced him to bear the weight of the crossbeam that Jesus could no longer carry. This man, who had likely come to Jerusalem for the Passover, was suddenly part of something bigger than any festival—the greatest story ever told, ever lived, ever conceived.

Simon was not the only person to play a vital part in this scene. Finally we have proof that the women were there too.

A large number of people followed him, including women who mourned and wailed for him. *Luke 23:27*

Yes, we see them. Among the "great multitude" (ESV) could be found "a lot of women" (CEV), all of them "grief-stricken" (NLT) as they "wrung their hands and wept for him" (PHILLIPS).

They apparently are not our named sisters—the three Marys, Martha, Joanna, Susanna, and the others. Rather, they are His followers from the Holy City. Women who perhaps had heard Him teach in the temple or watched Him heal the sick. Women who knew they were needed that morning and so came to do what they could.

Jesus turned and said to them, "Daughters of Jerusalem, . . ." *Luke 23:28*

Even shifting His position to look at them must have been an effort, given the seeping wounds, the deep bruising, the sheer exhaustion of putting one foot in front of the other as he trudged through the crowd of onlookers that pressed from every side.

When I walked through the Old City of Jerusalem on the Via Dolorosa—the "Way of Suffering," the path that Jesus took—I was struck by how steep it was and how narrow. The winding, uneven streets would have made His difficult journey even more perilous, and the steady uphill climb would have strained every muscle.

And yet He stopped to speak to the women.

Let me say that again. On the way to the cross, Jesus *stopped to speak to the women.* He sees us, beloved. He values us. He cherishes us.

On that day He spoke a word of prophecy to these daughters, preparing them for even harder days to come.

> ". . . do not weep for me; weep for yourselves and for your children." *Luke 23:28*

It was not that He wanted them to "stop crying" (ISV). Rather, He wanted them to know that their own suffering would soon require all these tears and more. "Cry for yourselves and your children" (CEB), Jesus told them.

> "For the time will come when you will say, 'Blessed are the childless women, the wombs that never bore and the breasts that never nursed!'" *Luke 23:29*

Only a woman could fully grasp the terrifying thought of barren women feeling "happy, fortunate, and to be envied" (AMPC) or "those who never gave birth or nursed babies" (NIrV) being called blessed.

> ". . . 'they will say to the mountains, "Fall on us!" and to the hills, "Cover us!"'" *Luke 23:30*

These faithful women surely recognized the ominous words from the prophet Hosea[41] and shuddered to think *they* would be the ones to "plead with the hills, 'Bury us'" (NLT)! This was a measure of mercy on the Lord's part, reminding them, warning them. To the end His mind and heart were attuned to the needs of others.

> Two other men, both criminals, were also led out with him to be executed. *Luke 23:32*

Unlike our blameless Savior, these were "wicked men" (WYC), guilty of their crimes and sentenced to be "put to death with Jesus" (CEV).

> When they came to the place called the Skull, . . .
> *Luke 23:33*

Yes, we know about this place, called Calvary in Latin and Golgotha in Hebrew. If you visit the Garden Tomb outside the walls of the Old City in Jerusalem today, you'll be shown the large rocky outcropping shaped like a "head bone" (WE). The scene looks nothing like the paintings we've seen—tall, grassy hills with three tidy crosses—and altogether like a place of death.

> . . . they crucified him there, along with the criminals—one on his right, the other on his left.
> *Luke 23:33*

Jesus was nailed to the heavy crossbeam, which weighed as much as a hundred pounds.[42] Then He was lifted up to the vertical beam, which was already in place, where possibly hundreds had been executed before Him.

Jesus did not hold Himself apart from the men beside Him or from the crowd that stared up at Him. Instead, He prayed for them.

> Jesus said, "Father, forgive them, for they do not know what they are doing." *Luke 23:34*

His first spoken word from the cross was *Father.*

It's comforting to know that Jesus was aware of His Father's abiding presence. He was not alone, not yet. His Father was there, and He was listening as Jesus offered a prayer of forgiveness *for the people who were crucifying Him.*

Let that sink in for a moment. He did not pray to be delivered from His pain. He did not pray for a swift end to His suffering. He did not pray for His Father to strike down Judas or Pilate or Herod or Caiaphas or anyone else who appeared to be responsible for His impending death.

Jesus alone was responsible. He hung on the cross willingly—no, *willfully.* However helpless He appeared to others, He was entirely in control. We know this because He had the strength to forgive them and then to go a step further and ask His Father to forgive them for killing His Son.

Only, only God. The One who offers His people grace at His own expense.

"Father, forgive these people!" (CEV). The Greek word translated "forgive" means "send away, leave alone, permit."[43] Jesus was asking God to let go of the punishment due His torturers and allow them to live. "They don't know what they are doing" (GNT), Jesus said, pleading on their behalf.

It was true. Even His own disciples didn't comprehend what was happening. If we're honest, that's our story too. We don't fully perceive how the death of One can pay for the sins of many. If we understood His grace in its fullness, we would live like people set free rather than like people trapped in our transgressions.

Jesus knew that those who hurled abuse at Him two thousand years ago were living in darkness, and He knows the same is true about critics who cast Him aside today. Nonetheless, Jesus remained on the cross for six agonizing hours, forgiving all of us for being desperately human and, like the Roman soldiers at His feet, remaining oblivious to the sacred sacrifice made on our behalf.

And they divided up his clothes by casting lots. *Luke 23:34*

At that world-shattering moment in human history, four soldiers were haggling over what Jesus was wearing as if His shredded clothing was of more value than the Lord Himself. They divided His garments "into four shares, one for each of them."[44] But His undergarment was "seamless, woven in one piece from top to bottom."[45] So rather than damage it, they cast lots for the garment,[46] then claimed their winnings.

They stripped Him bare. The Son of Man, revealed and reviled.

While those who'd followed Him wept, others simply stared.

The people stood watching, . . . *Luke 23:35*

Uninvolved, they merely "stood around" (WE), "calmly and leisurely" (AMPC) taking in the gruesome display, doing nothing more than "looking on" (YLT).

> . . . and the rulers even sneered at him. *Luke 23:35*

Hadn't they done enough? Determined to maximize His suffering, "the Jewish leaders laughed at Jesus" (ERV) and "derided him" (KJV). The Greek word literally means "to hold up the nose."[47] What an ugly sight they must have made!

> They said, "He saved others; let him save himself
> if he is God's Messiah, the Chosen One." *Luke
> 23:35*

They'd heard the accounts of dead bodies being raised to life. "He saved others, didn't he?" (ERV), they said for their mutual amusement. "Let's see him save himself!" (MSG).

The moment the rulers were done taunting Him, the Roman soldiers started making sport of Him, holding up sponges dipped in wine vinegar. Though it was a common drink among soldiers, sour wine mixed with water sounds anything but refreshing.

Like the Jewish leaders, the soldiers made the same challenge.

> . . . "If you are the king of the Jews, save yourself."
> *Luke 23:37*

But He didn't save Himself. He saved us. It took every minute on the cross to do so. They might have cut off His head or hanged Him with a rope or thrust a sword through His heart. All three methods would have taken His life quickly. But He *gave* His life so you and I and millions more might live, which surely required far more time and a far greater sacrifice.

> There was a written notice above him, which read:
> THIS IS THE KING OF THE JEWS. *Luke 23:38*

The "signboard was nailed to the cross" (TLB), prepared by Pilate himself, noting the charge against Him.[48] The chief priests had protested, "Do not write 'The King of the Jews,' but that this man claimed to be king of the Jews."[49] To which Pilate had answered, "What I have written, I have written."[50] This was not a crudely drawn sign but an official one "in letters of Greek, and Latin, and Hebrew" (DRA). Today when you drive through Jerusalem, many signs are in English, Arabic, and Hebrew for the same reason: so every passerby can read them.

As if the Lord were not sufficiently abused, another mocking voice chimed in.

> One of the criminals who hung there hurled insults at
> him: "Aren't you the Messiah? Save yourself and us!"
> *Luke 23:39*

A third time for the same challenge—"Prove it by saving yourself"—with an added request: "and us, too, while you're at it!" (NLT).

> But the other criminal rebuked him. "Don't you fear
> God," he said, "since you are under the same sentence?"
> *Luke 23:40*

I'm thinking this exchange was not shouted rapid fire but ground out with great difficulty. These men were suffering too, having surely been flogged for their crimes as Jesus had been. "Have you no fear of God?" (CJB), the second criminal asked the first, "seeing you are under the same condemnation?" (NKJV).

Whatever his crime, the second man feared God and knew that He hung beside him. The sincerity of the man's words reveals the inclination of his heart.

> "We are punished justly, for we are getting what our deeds deserve. But this man has done nothing wrong."
> *Luke 23:41*

This unnamed criminal was light-years ahead of most people. He realized he was a sinner: "you and I are guilty" (ERV). He understood the penalty for sin: "we deserve to die for our evil deeds" (TLB). And he knew Jesus was free of sin and so could free others from their sin: "this man never did anything wrong in his life" (PHILLIPS). It's the gospel in two sentences, spoken by a condemned man hanging from an execution stake.

> Then he said, "Jesus, remember me when you come into your kingdom." *Luke 23:42*

Remember me, Lord. A worthy request, humble and contrite, followed by an acknowledgment of where Jesus was headed: "when You come in Your kingly glory!" (AMPC). Literally, in the Greek, "the kingdom of you!"[51]

> Jesus answered him, "Truly I tell you, today you will be with me in paradise." *Luke 23:43*

Even when He was in agony, Jesus did not forgo His compassion for others. "I assure you" (AMP), Jesus said. "This is a solemn promise" (TLB). No need to describe "God's garden of paradise" (WE) for this man. Being with Jesus would be more than enough.

"Today you will be with me in paradise" (NIrV). Spoken to one sinner nailed to a cross. Spoken to many sinners nailed to their past. Spoken to all of us who long for hope and a future.

Seven

At the cross, her station keeping,
Stood the mournful mother weeping,
Where He hung, the dying Lord;
For her soul of joy bereavèd,
Bowed with anguish, deeply grievèd,
Felt the sharp and piercing sword.

—Translated by Edward Caswall,
"At the Cross Her Station Keeping," 1849

At the Cross Her
Station Keeping

*M*ary could hardly bear to look at her son, yet she couldn't take her eyes off Him. The face she'd scrubbed clean a thousand times was almost unrecognizable, so misshapen were His features. His head fell limp to the side, and His eyes were barely open, encrusted with blood and filth.

Near the cross of Jesus stood his mother, . . . *John 19:25*

She'd heard Him make a promise to the condemned man who hung beside Him. Could her son still hear? Still speak?

We can almost feel Mary's heart breaking and sense her thoughts, her emotions. Perhaps she remembered David weeping for his son—*"My son, my son Absalom! If only I had died instead of you"*[1]—and then nodded to herself, a fresh spate of tears running down her cheeks. Mary surely knew she never could have survived the scourging, the beating, the torturous crown of thorns. But, like any mother, she would have tried. For her son, she would have tried.

Her sister was there, perhaps resting a hand on her shoulder, offering unspoken comfort. On this terrible day—worse than any she'd ever imagined—Mary no doubt drew strength from God above and from the women who remained by her side.

> . . . his mother's sister, . . . *John 19:25*

The Lord's "aunt" (TLB) is not named here in John. Over the centuries some scholars have identified her as Salome, in part because a woman named Salome was present at the cross on Friday and at Jesus's grave on Sunday morning. But to assume that Salome was Mary's sister would rest "on supposition built on supposition and cannot be held as any more than a possibility."[2] However, we can be very certain of one thing: her nearness in this wretched scene assures us this unnamed woman cared deeply for Mary and would not let her suffer alone.

When my mother-in-law passed away while I was en route to a weekend conference, I immediately reached out to my closest friends who are also speakers, asking for their prayers. It's deeply instinctive, the need to share our grief, to seek solace from those who know us best and fully understand the situation. My friends buoyed my spirits just as Mary's sister must have comforted her.

On the crowded, dirty thoroughfare outside the city walls, strangers walked by her nephew, Jesus, hanging on the cross and gaped at Him, mocked Him, and degraded Him. She surely felt as helpless as Mary. And yet together these sisters stood and withstood. They didn't crouch in fear, they didn't turn their backs, they didn't slump on the ground in defeat, and they assuredly didn't walk away. They stood.

God calls us to do the same. To stand. To believe. To wait. To trust. "Therefore, my dear brothers and sisters, stand firm. Let nothing move you. Always give yourselves fully to the work of the Lord, because you know that your labor in the Lord is not in vain."[3]

Help us stand and withstand, Father. Help us be like these women.

Earlier we saw four soldiers casting lots. Now we'll watch "four women keeping faith."[4] Others were present, but these four stood especially close to the cross. Supporting one another. Supporting their Savior.

Along with Mary and her sister stood yet another Mary.

. . . Mary the wife of Clopas, . . . *John 19:25*

The fact that we're given her name is noteworthy. And we're grateful to know who her husband was, just to keep all the Marys straight. Clopas was an Israelite, whose only claim to fame was being the husband of this particular Mary. No small thing, considering she must have been a woman of deep faith and strong loyalty, based on her presence that day.

One more brave woman stood among them.

. . . and Mary Magdalene. *John 19:25*

Famous or infamous, she was a woman to be reckoned with. No listing of children and no mention of a husband suggest that Mary was an independent woman of some means, allowing her a measure of freedom rare in that day. Mary Magdalene traveled with the followers of Christ, several of whom shared her spirit-filled history.

Luke's gospel gives us a glimpse of her past.

> The Twelve were with him, and also some women who had been cured of evil spirits and diseases: Mary (called Magdalene) . . . *Luke 8:1–2*

These "certain women" (kjv) who were "in their company" (msg) were rather, um, *special.* They were females "from whom he had cast out demons or whom he had healed" (tlb). You'll recognize the Greek word for "cure"—*therapeuó*⁵—as the source of our modern word *therapeutic.*

Rather than music therapy or art therapy, Jesus excelled at *demon therapy,* delivering those who were tormented by "wicked spirits" (wyc). Interesting that the Lord cured demon possession in the same way He healed "illnesses" (cjb) and "infirmities" (esv): efficiently and effectively. Jesus "drove out the spirits with a word and healed all the sick."⁶ One word and these women were made whole, made new. No wonder they followed Him!

Mary Magdalene was known by her hometown, "the city of Magdala" (amp). The place is little more than rubble today, barely noticeable "on the coast of the Sea of Galilee near Tiberias."⁷ Many writers and artists have portrayed Mary Magdalene as a harlot, but the Bible never calls her that (trust me, I've looked!). What the Word *does* tell us is that she was once possessed.

> . . . from whom seven demons had come out; . . .
> *Luke 8:2*

Seven is the number of perfection or completion. Mary Magdalene had been filled to the brim with those "seven evil spirits" (phillips). Her deliverance isn't described beyond this assurance that "seven demons had been expelled" (ampc). The end.

As one of Jesus's most faithful followers, Mary Magdalene is mentioned by name *fourteen times* across all four gospel accounts. Extraordinary for any biblical character, but especially for a female in that culture. Now she stood with this impressive group of women—loyal, fearless, willing to do whatever was necessary to support their beloved Rabbi, even if it meant watching every agonizing minute of His execution.

Ancient tradition also places Martha and Mary of Bethany at the cross.[8] Certainly they were worthy of being present. They'd listened to His teaching, provided Him with lodging and meals, and anointed Him with oil of spikenard. Since Jesus loved both women and they worshiped Him in return, it's no stretch to imagine the Bethany sisters being there.

All around them were women who shared their faith, gazing at the cross from beneath their linen head coverings, unable to contain their grief, standing as close as they dared. When an enemy of the state was crucified, it was unsafe for family and friends to tarry nearby lest they be given the same terrible punishment for their innocent support of the condemned.[9] These women were brave indeed, risking death to behold His sacrifice.

It's one thing to see a loved one quietly pass from this world to the next. It's quite another to be present at a brutal execution, watching a beloved friend writhe in agony, struggling for every breath.

Could I watch You suffer, Lord? Could I stand so near?

Roman crosses were no more than nine feet tall, so the feet of the condemned would have been about a yard above the ground.[10] That meant Jesus could see the women's expressions and hear their anguished voices.

"Were you there when they crucified my Lord?" These women

had an answer. They were there. They were present. They were faithful. They didn't desert their Lord, as many had. If they looked away, we have no record of it. Even though their tears could not cleanse His wounds, the women were there. Even though their prayers could not stanch His bleeding, the women were there.

One commentator, reporting the reality of that era, wrote that women were "not highly regarded in Jewish society."[11] Even so, they were highly regarded by God. He observed their compassion, noted their courage, and treasured them as His daughters.

From the cross Jesus fixed His gaze on the woman who loved Him most.

> When Jesus saw his mother there, . . . *John 19:26*

The Son of God had looked into Mary's eyes as a nursing infant and walked toward her outstretched arms as a toddling child. Now He watched her weeping in despair, a widow about to lose her firstborn son.

How did You bear it, Lord? How did she?

Next to Mary stood His beloved disciple, John—the only one of the Eleven named among the witnesses that day at Golgotha.

> . . . and the disciple whom he loved standing nearby, . . .
> *John 19:26*

Looking at both of them, Jesus finally spoke.

> . . . he said to her, "Woman, here is your son," . . . *John 19:26*

We sense the tenderness in His voice. "Dear woman" (NCV) or "dear lady" (ISV) captures it best. It's a personal word, a relational word, often translated as "wife."[12] His love for His mother was abundantly clear. Aware of the invisible sword piercing her heart, Jesus tended to her wound in the best way possible—assuring her that she was not alone, that she would be cared for, provided for, and loved.

"Behold, thy son!" (ASV). Perhaps the apostle John was physically supporting Mary lest she collapse in grief. They were both close enough to hear Jesus above the murmuring crowd. "This man is now your son" (CEV), Jesus said.

Did Mary's heart skip a beat? There's a difference between knowing someone is dying and truly accepting that death is imminent. Perhaps for Mary that reality became painfully clear at that moment. She had a new son, because the son of her womb would soon be gone.

Jesus spoke directly to John as well.

> . . . and to the disciple, "Here is your mother." *John 19:27*

The Lord once said those who followed Him were His true family.[13] This loving gesture at the cross must have reassured Mary that He still treasured her as His mother. He had not abandoned her and never would. Through this act of loving-kindness, "Jesus fulfilled one of the greatest commandments in the Torah: the commandment to honor one's parents."[14]

With her husband, Joseph, apparently no longer living and her resources likely meager, Mary could not manage alone.

"Protect and provide for her" (AMP), Jesus instructed John. "She is now your mother" (CEV).

> From that time on, this disciple took her into his home.
> *John 19:27*

Since this is from John's gospel, written near the end of his earthly life, he could confirm that the Lord's final request was honored. The word *home* isn't in the original Greek; it's only implied. But John did something more tender still. He took Mary not only into his house but also into his heart. "From that moment the disciple accepted her as his own mother" (MSG), just as the Lord intended.

Then at high noon—the sixth hour of the Jewish day—darkness fell.

> From noon until three in the afternoon darkness came
> over all the land. *Matthew 27:45*

Centuries earlier "Moses stretched out his hand toward the sky, and total darkness covered all Egypt for three days."[15] In a similar way, God stretched out His hand, and total darkness covered all Israel "from noon until three o'clock in the afternoon" (CJB). Whether the darkness arrived all at once or moved across the hills and plains of Judea like an approaching storm, "the whole earth was dark" (CEB) for *three full hours.* The black of night covered the light of day, even as the Light of the World bore the darkness of our sin.

Perhaps the crowd fell silent, afraid to move, dreading the

possibility of what might happen next. Were all ten plagues about to be visited upon Israel? Locusts and boils and far worse?

"Blackness hints at the deep judgment that was taking place."[16] Beneath the thick blanket of darkness, Jesus was held accountable for the countless sins of God's people. Those unmentionable things we did last month, last year, last decade? That thoughtless act we're going to do next week? Jesus paid the penalty for every one of those sins. All of them, for all time.

The punishment we just witnessed—the beating, the flogging, the mocking, the crown of thorns—was only the start. The worst of His torture came in the dark, when no one could see. Just as Satan tempted Him in the wilderness,[17] perhaps he tempted Jesus now under the cover of darkness. We can only imagine the evil schemes he used against the Lord to keep Him from completing His redemptive work. "For we wrestle not against flesh and blood, but against principalities, against powers, against the rulers of the darkness of this world."[18]

For three more hours Jesus wrestled with the weight of our sin, with the designs of the Enemy, and with the silence from heaven.

When the end came, His anguished voice pierced the darkness.

> About three in the afternoon Jesus cried out in a loud voice, *"Eli, Eli, lema sabachthani?"* (which means "My God, my God, why have you forsaken me?"). *Matthew 27:46*

Alone. Jesus was alone.

The spiritual and emotional impact of the Son's complete separation from the Father is beyond the grasp of our finite minds.

"Why have you abandoned me?" (NCV), Jesus cried out.

No reply.

And yet, look how His words, drawn from the psalms,[19] begin: "My God, my God." In the original Greek, it's "God of me, God of me."[20] Despite the silence from heaven, Jesus knew God was still His Father. "Even in the depth of his sufferings God was his God."[21]

What a word for us, beloved. Even when God seems far away, even when God is silent, He is still our Father, He is still our God, and He is still at work in our lives.

> Later, knowing that everything had now been finished, and so that Scripture would be fulfilled, Jesus said, "I am thirsty." *John 19:28*

Again His words were drawn from the psalms: "For my thirst they gave me vinegar to drink."[22] So Jesus, in obedience to His Word, said, "I thirst" (AMPC). Even the smallest prophecy came to fruition in Him.

> Immediately one of them ran and got a sponge. He filled it with wine vinegar, put it on a staff, and offered it to Jesus to drink. *Matthew 27:48*

Water would have been better to relieve His parched mouth. Yet Jesus drank.

When he had received the drink, Jesus said, "It is finished." *John 19:30*

Not "I am finished," but "*it* is finished." His supreme sacrifice was over. His mighty work of redemption was done. He came to earth to do the will of His Father, and He had accomplished that. Every pen stroke of His Word was fulfilled by Jesus's obedience.

In Greek the word translated as "finished" means "to bring to an end, complete, fulfill."[23] By His death Jesus abolished the ceremonial Law and all its obligations, stamping them *paid in full.*

At last He could leave behind His ravaged body and put His spirit in safe hands.

Jesus called out with a loud voice, . . . *Luke 23:46*

He "gave a great cry" (PHILLIPS) with a supernatural strength accessible to Him now that He and the Father were reunited. This is what He shouted:

. . . "Father, into your hands I commit my spirit." *Luke 23:46*

The last words He spoke were from the first line of Psalm 31:5, written by His ancestor David a thousand years earlier. To the very end Jesus demonstrated His sovereignty. When He said, "I put my life in your hands!" (ERV), He alone chose the time of His death. His life was not taken but given, then entrusted to His Father. "Into thine hands I commend my spirit" (GNV).

When he had said this, he breathed his last. *Luke 23:46*

His head slumped forward, and His arms, which were stretched across the wooden crosspiece, went limp as Jesus "gave up the ghost" (ASV) and "breathed forth the spirit" (YLT). Beautiful, poetic phrasing, but the translation closest to the original Greek is "He expired" (AMPC).

Yes. It is finished.

Those words land in my heart like a stone. We know how He died and why He died, but heavenly Father, did it have to be like this? So much pain and anguish! Is that what it took to break our yoke of sin?

Yes. And it is finished.

At that moment . . . *Matthew 27:51*

No sooner had the breath left His body than "lo!" (WYC) a remarkable chain of events was put into motion. "Suddenly" (ISV) some distance away at the temple in Jerusalem, "behold" (KJV) a miracle.

. . . the curtain of the temple was torn in two from top to bottom. *Matthew 27:51*

Imagine fine linen cloth, thickly woven with blue, purple, and scarlet yarn, summarily "rent in twain" (KJV). If you've ever tried to tear, say, denim with your bare hands, you know what a feat of strength this was. No one but God Himself could have ripped the inner veil in two, starting at the top and tearing "all the way down to the bottom" (ICB).

Not only did this allow access to the Most Holy Place, where only the high priest had been permitted to go, and only once a year,[24] but the torn curtain also invited "open access to God."[25] No more separation. No more blood sacrifices. No more fear of death.

Because of Jesus, we can stand in God's holy presence and live!

And that was only the beginning.

The earth shook, the rocks split . . . *Matthew 27:51*

Oh my. "The earth did quake, and the rocks were rent" (YLT). Jerusalem lies on a major fault line that rivals the San Andreas fault and has suffered many damaging earthquakes over the centuries. But none quite like this one when Jesus struck "the fatal blow . . . to the devil's kingdom."[26]

. . . and the tombs broke open. *Matthew 27:52*

Picture thousands of graves scattered across the Mount of Olives since the time of David suddenly breaking apart. To onlookers it must have appeared "the graves did open themselves" (GNV).

While the earth was quaking, the guards were shaking.

When the centurion and those with him who were guarding Jesus saw the earthquake and all that had happened, they were terrified, . . . *Matthew 27:54*

If these men were able to see what was happening, then the darkness had vanished as quickly as it had appeared, just in time for them to watch the solid ground buckle and huge rocks split open. No wonder they were "extremely frightened" (LEB).

> . . . and exclaimed, "Surely he was the Son of God!"
> *Matthew 27:54*

When the Roman soldiers blurted out, "This was certainly God's Son" (CEB), you can be sure those were not their own words. Rather, they were provided by the Holy Spirit, since "no one can say, 'Jesus is Lord,' except by the Holy Spirit."[27]

Undone, the crowd "returned to their homes, beating their breasts,"[28] a sign of repentance. After the darkness and then the earthquake, they had seen quite enough of this Jesus.

Now that He was gone, His followers no longer had a reason to tarry at the cross. His body did not belong to them. Pontius Pilate decided when and how the remains of the condemned were handled. Some bodies were taken down and left on the ground. Others were placed on a trash heap,[29] further extending the cruel and inhumane treatment inflicted by Rome.

Even so, the women remained.

They were farther away from the cross by this point in the afternoon. Perhaps they, too, had started for home but couldn't bear the thought of leaving Him and instead chose to stay.

> Many women were there, watching from a distance.
> *Matthew 27:55*

We don't know how many women were on hand. "Numerous" (AMPC) or "quite a few" (MSG) doesn't tell us much. Nor do we have any measure of how "afar off" (KJV) they were, "beholding" (ASV) the chaotic scene.

Matthew reminds his readers who these women were and why they'd come.

> They had followed Jesus from Galilee to care for his needs. *Matthew 27:55*

I love the phrase "ministering to Him" (AMP). As if they were returning the favor, using the gifts they'd been given by Him.

> Among them were Mary Magdalene, Mary the mother of James and Joseph, and the mother of Zebedee's sons. *Matthew 27:56*

Mary Magdalene is given pride of place here—older, wiser, devoted to her Lord. When Jesus set Mary free from her demons, her soul was His forever. By her side was Mary, the mother of James the disciple and his brother Joses or Joseph—same person, different spelling. And Salome, the wife of Zebedee and mother to his sons.[30]

I know. It's hard to keep all these women straight. What's amazing is that they're even mentioned. All four gospel writers captured the Lord's desire to honor these women—listing them, often naming them, and anchoring them in their families and communities.

As we shift to the book of John, we sense the forward motion in this journey. The sadness, the darkness, was receding as the women prepared, however unknowingly, for Easter.

> Now it was the day of Preparation, and the next day was
> to be a special Sabbath. *John 19:31*

The Sabbath would begin at sunset, about six o'clock.[31] At the scene of the execution, the legs of the two criminals were broken to hasten their deaths—a mercy of sorts—because the Jewish leaders didn't want the bodies to remain on the crosses after the start of the Sabbath.

> But when they came to Jesus and found that he was
> already dead, they did not break his legs. *John 19:33*

This, too, was an unwitting mercy and a fulfillment of prophecy: "He [the LORD] protects all his bones, not one of them will be broken."[32] Before Jesus's grieving followers could breathe a sigh of relief that His body was spared, a soldier reached for his lance, determined to make the Lord's death a certainty.

> One of the soldiers pierced Jesus' side with a spear,
> bringing a sudden flow of blood and water. *John 19:34*

A line from a hymn comes to mind: "Sorrow and love flow mingled down."[33] *Yes.* Great sorrow. Even greater love.

His body was not the only thing pierced. Surely Mary's heart also felt the point of that spear as she looked on in horror. What could be more devastating than watching her child executed for a crime He did not commit and then seeing His lifeless body mistreated?

This was God's Son and hers. Even at that terrible hour, Mary did not forsake Him.

The prophet Zechariah foretold this too: "They will look on me, the one they have pierced, and they will mourn for him as one mourns for an only child, and grieve bitterly for him as one grieves for a firstborn son."[34]

In the hours that followed, John may have escorted Mary to his lodging place, since we have no record of her presence in the next scene.

> As evening approached, there came a rich man from Arimathea, named Joseph, who had himself become a disciple of Jesus. *Matthew 27:57*

Twilight lengthened the shadows as Joseph, "one of Jesus' followers" (TLB), appeared. He was "a prominent member of the Council,"[35] a member of the Sanhedrin, so we can be certain "his discipleship was secret."[36] Even so, this wealthy man, "who was himself waiting for the kingdom of God, went boldly to Pilate and asked for Jesus' body."[37]

Never mind Joseph's power and wealth. His request took a lot of courage. Wisely, he brought with him another man who was also a member of the Jewish ruling council[38] and a follower of Christ. His name was Nicodemus, and he came bearing gifts.

> Nicodemus brought a mixture of myrrh and aloes, about seventy-five pounds. *John 19:39*

You read that correctly. *Seventy-five pounds.* Not pure nard, like Mary of Bethany's pound of ointment, but still costly. And heavy. Nicodemus arrived "bearing a medley of myrrh and aloes" (WYC), a generous offering.

> Taking Jesus' body, the two of them wrapped it, with
> the spices, in strips of linen. This was in accordance with
> Jewish burial customs. *John 19:40*

Rather than covering His body with a single burial shroud, they "bound it in linen wrappings" (AMP). "It." This was no longer Jesus—only His lifeless body. Even though He was killed by Jews and mockingly called King of the Jews, Joseph and Nicodemus still followed "the burial custom of the Jews" (ESV).

> At the place where Jesus was crucified, there was a gar-
> den, . . . *John 19:41*

The story of humankind began in a garden, and so to a garden we return. Don't you love how the Lord fits everything together in a billion-piece puzzle only He can assemble? The first man and woman were born in the Garden of Eden. Now all God's people can be born again because of what was about to happen in this garden, this "grove of trees" (TLB) near the cross.

Where life became death, death will become life.

A sense of excitement is building inside me. *Is it Sunday yet? We're so ready, Lord!*

> . . . and in the garden a new tomb, in which no one had
> ever been laid. *John 19:41*

Not a natural cave then, but a tomb "cut out of solid rock" (AMP) at some expense. "A new sepulcher" (GNV) that had "never been used before" (EXB). Every detail matters. The new, unused tomb meant the Lord's flesh would not come in contact with anything corrupt. Even in death this Jewish law was observed.

> . . . [Joseph] placed it in his own new tomb that he
> had cut out of the rock. *Matthew 27:60*

The grave is identified as belonging to Joseph of Arimathea. Was he ill, making preparations for his death? Or was he the sort of man who planned ahead? Whatever reason Joseph might offer, we know this was God's perfect timing at work. A clean, empty tomb was needed for His Son, and here it was.

> He rolled a big stone in front of the entrance to the
> tomb and went away. *Matthew 27:60*

Instead of a round, globe-shaped stone, this was a large, flat disc, rolled into place along a downward groove cut into the ground in front of the tomb. Such a design made the stone easy to roll into place and almost impossible to move. Almost.

> The women who had come with Jesus from Galilee followed Joseph and saw the tomb and how his body was
> laid in it. *Luke 23:55*

Really, have you ever seen such perseverance? They stayed and they stayed and they stayed. This is one of the most important lessons these women teach us. Wherever He leads, follow Jesus. Whatever pain you are enduring, keep your eyes on Jesus. Even when hope seems gone, stay close to Jesus.

> Mary Magdalene and the other Mary were sitting there
> opposite the tomb. *Matthew 27:61*

Like Mary of Bethany sitting shivah, Mary Magdalene and the other Mary—the one with the sons whose names both start with the letter *J*—were seated across from the closed tomb. Since "no mourning was permitted for those executed under Roman law,"[39] the women had to grieve in silence. No loud wailing, as was the custom.

Although the Lord had promised His followers He would rise again in three days, it must have been hard to see past the truth right in front of them: a tomb with the body of a young man who died in His early thirties. Focused on the inescapable facts before them, the women could not fathom the joy that would be theirs on the third day.

Jesus had repeatedly told His disciples this was going to happen. He'd also shown them resurrection was possible by raising Lazarus and others before him. Yet even when the evidence is clear, the most faithful among us, like these women, sometimes miss the truth. We believe only what we can understand or explain, only what seems possible, only what we can see.

Help us take the leap of faith that Easter requires, Lord. Help us believe.

Though Nicodemus had already anointed the Lord's body with myrrh and aloes, the women wanted to do their part. But the sun was setting, and the Sabbath was about to begin. Nothing more could be done at the tomb.

> Then they went home and prepared spices and per-
> fumes. *Luke 23:56*

With little time left before *Shabbat*, the women quickly gathered the myrrh and other natural unguents needed for burial, mindful of the approaching darkness, careful to honor God's Word.

> But they rested on the Sabbath in obedience to the commandment. *Luke 23:56*

How the waiting must have grieved them! Wanting to visit His resting place, wanting to pay their respects, wanting to anoint His body with "some sweet-smelling spices for his burial" (CEV).

Considering the large stone that Joseph of Arimathea had rolled in front of the Lord's tomb, I'm curious how the women planned to get inside. But they were not thinking about obstacles. They were thinking about Jesus.

Our sisters counted the hours until Saturday at sundown. Only then, after a full day of keeping the Sabbath holy, were they free to make their move.

> When the Sabbath was over, Mary Magdalene, Mary the mother of James, and Salome . . . *Mark 16:1*

Are these women coming into focus for you? We're given no physical descriptions of them in the Bible. No body types, no hair colors, no skin tones, no prominent features. If we're not careful, we might paint them all with the same brush.

Yet God saw them as unique, one of a kind. Not based on their outward appearance, which is often our main focus, but on their hearts, His only focus. God looks at us not as blondes or brunettes or redheads or silver-haired saints, not as tall or short or big or small, not as gorgeous or pretty or average or homely. Those distinctions are human, not divine, and meaningless in the end.

What matters to God is the relationship we have with Him.

The simplicity of it steals my breath. *That's it, Lord?* That's it.

So we turn to our first-century role models and watch them express their love for Him through their actions on Saturday evening, prompted by the Holy Spirit. Apparently they didn't think they had sufficient oils and ointments on hand, so off to the night market they went.

> . . . bought spices so that they might go to anoint Jesus' body. *Mark 16:1*

Almost every English translation uses the word *bought* or *purchased,* so it's clear they went shopping. In modern Jerusalem when the Sabbath ends, the shops open again for a short time. In much the same way, in ancient Jerusalem shoppers might have found a market stall offering silks and embroidered fabrics, another selling fruits and herbs, and a third displaying the "fragrant spices" (LEB) our sisters were looking for.

Task accomplished, the women returned home to sleep as best they could, planning to rise at dawn and hurry to the tomb.

The sad news? These faithful souls still expected to find a dead body in that tomb the next morning. The glad news? They were determined to care for the Lord. They had not forgotten Him, not abandoned Him, and not denied knowing Him.

For now, they could do nothing but wait for the morning light to usher in a new day. "Out of this thickest midnight, who can tell what dawn shall yet arise?"[40]

Eight

I know that my Redeemer lives;
What comfort this sweet sentence gives!
He lives, He lives, who once was dead;
He lives, my ever-living Head.

—Samuel Medley, "I Know That
My Redeemer Lives," 1775

I Know That My
Redeemer Lives

*T*he women woke before dawn, quickly dressed, and
gathered their fresh spices in woven-reed baskets.
Finally the time had come.

> Very early on the first day of the week, just after
> sunrise, . . . *Mark 16:2*

The hour is described in precise detail—"very early in the
morning" (WE), "just as the sun was coming up" (CEV). John's gospel adds "while it was still dark,"[1] capturing that brief moment
when the heavens were still a velvety dark blue and only a hint of
daylight brushed the eastern sky.

I'm not usually up and about that early, but on mornings
when I wake before dawn, I find myself gazing out our kitchen
window, awed by the swiftly changing colors. The whole day
stands on tiptoe, awash in pinks and yellows, waiting for the sun
to crest the horizon. It's only a matter of minutes, but oh those
minutes! Charged with anticipation, filled with hope.

A new day. Anything might happen.

Scientists are quick to remind us that the sun doesn't actually rise. We, on our spinning planet, are the ones moving in the direction of the sun. That's exactly what the women of Easter were doing: moving in the direction of the Son.

> . . . they were on their way to the tomb . . . *Mark 16:2*

Light hurrying to meet the darkness. *Life* hastening to find the dead.

Was there ever such a morning in the history of the world?

Mark's gospel tells us that Mary Magdalene, Mary the mother of James, and Salome went spice shopping on Saturday night.[2] But in this verse we're simply told "they came to the tomb" (LEB). Shall we assume it's the same three women?

Luke's gospel talks about "the women who had come with Jesus from Galilee"[3] at the end of one chapter and then begins the next with "the women took the spices they had prepared."[4] If Luke meant all the women from Galilee, that would have been quite a number, and Mary of Nazareth would likely have been counted among them.

Matthew's gospel mentions only two women: "Mary Magdalene, and the other Mary, came to see the sepulcher."[5] And John's gospel names just one woman: "Mary Magdalene went to the tomb."[6]

We know the Bible is the very definition of truth. So how can we explain these differing accounts? Simply put, they offer four points of view of the same scene. If a woman isn't mentioned by name, it doesn't mean she wasn't there—only that she wasn't noted in Scripture.

If someone asks you, "Who did you see at church on Sunday?" you might mention two or three people by name, even though dozens or hundreds were there. You *saw* them but didn't include them in your comments.

I think John featured Mary Magdalene because, before the morning was over, she was the one who proclaimed the good news to the disciples. Matthew probably added "the other Mary" since she remained with Mary Magdalene at the tomb on Friday evening. Mark and Luke didn't include any names at this point in their accounts, yet—and this is what matters—*all four gospel writers agreed the witnesses were women.*

Think of it! Jesus Christ—the Holy One, the King of kings, the Savior of the world—was conquering death *at that very moment.* The dozen men who'd traveled everywhere with Him were nowhere to be seen. But the women—the few, the faithful, the resourceful—were headed to the grave for one simple reason.

The Lord wanted them there.

Our Sovereign God didn't leave a single moment of His Son's resurrection to chance. He knew from before the beginning of time that these women would be the first to know, the first to see. The male disciples weren't neglecting their duties. *They weren't called to be there.*

God chose women to serve as His witnesses this day. Yes, He did.

Right on cue our sisters passed through the Damascus Gate, bound for the garden tomb.

> . . . and they asked each other, "Who will roll the stone
> away from the entrance of the tomb?" *Mark 16:3*

Clearly, they couldn't manage this herculean task themselves. "Who will move the stone for us?" (ERV), they wondered. In a morning full of miracles, this was the first one.

> But when they looked up, they saw that the stone, which was very large, had been rolled away. *Mark 16:4*

Make no mistake, it was "exceeding great" (ASV), "a huge stone!" (CEV). Four to five feet in diameter and perhaps a foot thick, it was far too heavy for these women to roll aside. In his gospel, Matthew describes how this miraculous move occurred before the women even arrived at the grave.

> There was a violent earthquake, for an angel of the Lord came down from heaven and, going to the tomb, rolled back the stone and sat on it. *Matthew 28:2*

The earth shook and the rock rolled. The quake was "strong" (NCV), "severe" (NET), and "powerful" (NIrV), much like the earthquake on Good Friday, when "the rocks split and the tombs broke open."[7] Perhaps this was an aftershock, planned by God before the beginning of time.

By the time the women of Easter arrived at the garden tomb, the angel had found a new place to sit: inside the burial space.

> As they entered the tomb, they saw a young man dressed in a white robe sitting on the right side, . . . *Mark 16:5*

Archaeologists believe the entrance was no more than three feet high and two feet wide. The only way to enter was to assume a posture of humility—head bowed, torso bent. Our women were prepared to find a body, fragrant with myrrh, but they were not expecting an angel dressed in white.

His angelic robe wasn't the kind you hang on a bathroom door. It was "long, stately, sweeping" (AMPC) and blindingly bright.

> His appearance was like lightning, . . . *Matthew 28:3*

Lightning isn't subtle. It's startling, frightening, and, yes, electrifying. If you've always thought of angels as cherubic, think again. "He was vibrating with light" (VOICE). Oh my. "Shafts of lightning blazed from him" (MSG). Oh my.

> The guards were so afraid of him that they shook and became like dead men. *Matthew 28:4*

Their job was to guard a dead man's tomb, yet they were the ones who "fell into a dead faint" (NLT). As for the women, they were still on their feet, but barely.

> . . . they were alarmed. *Mark 16:5*

You can be certain they were "completely taken aback" (MSG) and duly "struck with terror" (AMPC)! Some people might have run for their lives. Not Mary Magdalene and the others who joined her that morning. However afraid they might have been, our sisters didn't leave. They also didn't look.

> In their fright the women bowed down with their faces to the ground, . . . *Luke 24:5*

Overcome, they "were awestruck and bowed down in worship" (MSG). With their foreheads pressed against their hands, the women could do nothing but wait and trust. Would this lightning-white being speak? Or would he strike them dead?

No wonder heavenly messengers often begin with these words:

> "Don't be alarmed," he said. *Mark 16:6*

The words "Be not afraid" (KJ21) were meant to calm their fast-beating hearts. Did the Marys exchange glances and then slowly inch their hands toward each other to bolster their courage? The angel assured them, "There is nothing to fear,"[8] but it's hard to stop shivering once you start.

His next words were a statement, not a question. The angel knew why they'd come and whom they were seeking.

> "You are looking for Jesus the Nazarene, who was crucified." *Mark 16:6*

Yes. All the vital facts are here. His name is Jesus. He hailed from Nazareth. And He is the One who was "killed on a cross" (ERV), who was "executed on the stake" (CJB), who was "hanged on the Tree" (OJB).

This is it. This is the moment.

All of creation held its breath.

> "He has risen!" *Mark 16:6*

Hallelujah! God be praised!

(I'm standing. Are you standing?)

This glorious truth has the power to transform everything and everyone, including us. His heavenly Father "raised him to life" (CEV). He who was dead is now alive forever!

Did the women lift their heads and then their arms in spontaneous praise? Or were they too stunned to move as they listened to the angel's next words in astonishment?

> "He is not here. See the place where they laid him."
> *Mark 16:6*

It was evident Jesus was not in the tomb. Still, the angel invited them to look. "You can see for yourselves that the place is empty" (MSG). The stone shelves around the inside walls of the tomb were indeed vacant.

No body. No Jesus. Thanks be to God!

Luke's gospel includes a parting reminder from the angel, making the most of a teachable moment.

> "Remember how he told you, while he was still with you
> in Galilee: 'The Son of Man must be delivered over to
> the hands of sinners, be crucified and on the third day
> be raised again.'" *Luke 24:6–7*

Who could forget such a remarkable prophecy? The worst possible thing, the best possible thing—both accomplished in three days. From the beginning Jesus knew how this week would unfold. His followers were only now starting to see the big picture.

Then they remembered his words. *Luke 24:8*

Of course. The prophecy Jesus had spoken in Galilee was coming true before their eyes. Sinful men had indeed nailed Him to a cross. And this was the third day, which could only mean . . .

The women must have turned to one another, eyes wide, mouths agape. *He truly has risen!*

Before they could respond, the angel gave them an assignment.

> "But go, tell his disciples and Peter, 'He is going ahead of
> you into Galilee. There you will see him, just as he told
> you.'" *Mark 16:7*

There was no longer a reason to hang around the empty garden tomb. With the angel's words ringing in their ears and resounding in their hearts, the women were on a mission: "Now go and give this message to his disciples" (GNT).

"Go"? Not a problem. These women were probably anxious to be gone. But "tell his followers" (ERV)? Not as easy. What would the women say? "We saw an angel! The tomb is empty! He is risen!" Would the disciples believe them without proof? After all, our sisters had yet to see the risen Lord.

> Trembling and bewildered, the women went out and
> fled from the tomb. *Mark 16:8*

They took off, "confused and shaking" (CEV), "distressed and terrified" (GNT). We get the picture. They freaked out. Who wouldn't? Still, their feet were moving, and their path was certain as they hurried through the streets of Jerusalem.

I wonder if they left behind their spices in the same way the Samaritan woman left behind her water jar?[9] No need for burial ointments now. He is *alive*!

At first glance it *almost* appears as if they ignored the angel's directive to go and tell:

> They said nothing to anyone, because they were afraid.
> *Mark 16:8*

Ah, but they wouldn't have mentioned this astounding news to just anyone who crossed their path that morning, right? The disciples had to be told first. The men were probably lodging nearby inside the city walls, crowded into a private residence with other believers. In any case, that's where the women headed.

> When they came back from the tomb, they told all these things to the Eleven and to all the others. *Luke 24:9*

Eleven disciples now, along with the other followers who remained faithful to Jesus. Our sisters breathlessly spilled out the events of the morning.

> It was Mary Magdalene, Joanna, Mary the mother of James, and the others with them who told this to the apostles. *Luke 24:10*

Mary Magdalene, the former demoniac, led the way. Isn't that just like our Lord? To entrust the least likely? To promote the least popular? To put to good use those who've weathered a bad season?

Of our trio of Marys, only Mary Magdalene had a shadow cast across her past, yet here she came, leading the women in proclaiming the tomb was empty.

How I wish I could tell you the disciples welcomed the news with open ears and open hearts. Alas, that's not what happened.

> But they did not believe the women, because their words seemed to them like nonsense. *Luke 24:11*

You read that right. "The apostles didn't believe a word of it" (MSG), certain what the women were saying was "an idle tale" (AMPC), "utter nonsense" (CJB), even a touch of "madness" (WYC). In truth, the apostles "thought they were making it all up" (MSG).

Well, I never. What sort of Easter morning was this?

The real one, my friend, full of disbelief, fear, and confusion. Could this outrageous resurrection story be true? Did a dead man really walk out of a tomb?

People are still seeking answers to those questions. That's why God's Word encourages us, "If someone asks about your hope as a believer, always be ready to explain it."[10] By all means, talk about His love, His mercy, His grace, and His compassion, but our hope is built entirely on His resurrection.

What the disciples needed at that hour was a risen Savior standing before them with nail-pierced hands. Then they would see for themselves and believe.

Soon, very soon.

Meanwhile, Mary Magdalene convinced Peter and the beloved disciple, John, to run with her back to the garden tomb and look for themselves. Peter and John saw the empty grave but no Jesus, the strips of linen but no Jesus. No angels, either.

Then the disciples went back to where they were staying. *John 20:10*

Mary Magdalene lingered behind, alone. She couldn't leave. Not until she was certain what had happened to Jesus. Of Mary's many admirable qualities—her strength, her courage, her willingness to lead—the one that mattered most was her faithfulness.

Now Mary stood outside the tomb crying. *John 20:11*

Bless her. The word *maudlin* comes from *Magdalene*—the name of this dear woman who couldn't stop weeping. Crushed in spirit, Mary Magdalene stared at the emptiness looming before her. The tomb, yes, but also her uncertain future. What if the Lord hadn't risen after all? Would evil prevail? Would her demons return?

After seeing Him suffer on the cross, now Mary had to face the awful possibility that, rather than a resurrection, His body had been taken.

As she wept, she bent over to look into the tomb and saw . . . *John 20:11–12*

Peter had seen only strips of linen and then "went away, wondering to himself what had happened."[11] But Mary Magdalene saw heavenly beings.

. . . two angels in white, seated where Jesus' body had been, one at the head and the other at the foot. *John 20:12*

This time our brave Mary M. didn't quake in fear or fall to her knees. The angels addressed her—not by name but by gender—and spoke directly to her sorrow.

> They asked her, "Woman, why are you crying?" *John 20:13*

Perhaps doubt had crept into Mary's heart. She'd heard He was risen, but she could not find Him. Jesus said He would return from the dead, but He was not there.

> "They have taken my Lord away," she said, "and I don't know where they have put him." *John 20:13*

Her answer was swift, though it must have pained her to confess the reason for her tears—"because they've taken away my Lord" (HCSB). Who were "they," Mary? Soldiers, graverobbers, priests? She was too heartbroken to explain further, undone by the sad reality—"I do not know where they have laid Him" (NASB).

When we're in pain, we often reveal the deepest truths. That's what Mary did when she said, "They have taken away my Lord's body!" (CEV). *My Lord.* So intimate, in the best sense. Jesus was not only her Savior. He was also her friend.

Lord, help us think of You as Mary did—as our dearest companion, our truest friend.

That's why Mary Magdalene remained at the tomb. Not out of duty, but out of love. The same love that kept Mary of Bethany at His feet. The same love that kept Mary of Nazareth at the cross.

The same love that stirs in our hearts and for the same reason—"We love because he first loved us."[12]

Mary Magdalene's deep and abiding love for Him was about to be rewarded.

At this, she turned around . . . *John 20:14*

At *what*? Did Mary hear an unexpected sound? Feel something brush against her shoulder? Or did she sense the presence of Someone else in the garden? While any or all of those things may have happened, the original Greek reads more like this: "After uttering these words" (VOICE) or "Having said this" (ESV). Yes, that makes sense. She simply finished speaking.

Then Mary "turned aback" (WYC) and discovered she was not alone.

. . . and saw Jesus standing there, . . . *John 20:14*

Our hearts stop. *He is risen, Mary! He is risen indeed!*

. . . but she did not realize that it was Jesus. *John 20:14*

What? How could Mary not see this was the man she'd served for years? Did her tears cloud her vision? Or had He changed so completely that she didn't recognize Him? Perhaps the Lord kept her in the dark a few moments longer for His good purposes.

At last He had a word for Mary Magdalene. He has the same word for us, sisters, and it's a beautiful word.

"Woman, . . ." *John 20:15*

Woman. The first word spoken by the risen Christ, meant for all His daughters throughout eternity. *Woman.* An assurance that we matter to Him, that we count for His kingdom. *Woman.* A term of respect. The very word He used when addressing His beloved mother from the cross. *Woman.*

". . . why are you crying?" *John 20:15*

I can tell you why *I'm* crying. *Because Jesus chose a woman.* He could have revealed His risen self first to any one of the Eleven, but He chose Mary Magdalene, a former demoniac, a midlife caregiver, a faithful follower. *A woman.*

Jesus knew why Mary was crying, just as He understands what makes us weep. Even so, He asked the same question the angels had put to her. Not to embarrass her, but to encourage her. *No need for tears, Mary. Not anymore.*

"Who is it you are looking for?" *John 20:15*

Jesus asked this second question on the heels of the first, helping her move past her tears so she could move past her fears. *He is not dead, Mary. Look! See!*

Thinking he was the gardener, . . . *John 20:15*

Hmm. Why did Mary think "he was the man in charge of the garden" (ERV)? Perhaps because she was *in* a garden—a logical conclusion, especially at that early hour. Though, to be honest, Mary wasn't thinking logically, since what she said next was pure foolishness.

> . . . she said, "Sir, if you have carried him away, tell
> me where you have put him, and I will get him."
> *John 20:15*

"Mister, if you took him" (MSG), she began—as if a gardener would have any reason to remove a corpse from a tomb—"just tell me where you put him; and I'll go and get him myself" (CJB). Really, Mary? You thought you could lift a grown man's dead body all by yourself? And carry it how far exactly?

In the depths of her grief, Mary Magdalene had lost the ability to see clearly, to think clearly. I understand. When my second brother, John, passed away only two years after Tom, and my oldest brother, Dave, nine months later, I was dumbstruck. *Not again, Lord. Not so soon.* All the things I should have, could have, would have done weighed on my heart until I thought it might burst. Logic? Reason? Common sense? Not when grief holds your heart captive.

In the darkness of her sorrow, Mary Magdalene needed someone to assure her that one day life would make sense again. That she would be dry eyed and in her right mind. That all was not lost.

Who better to tell her than her beloved Savior?

> Jesus said to her, "Mary." *John 20:16*

Imagine hearing His voice speak your name.

She turned toward him . . . *John 20:16*

All He needed to say was "Mary!" (NLT). She knew at once who stood behind her and "turned right round" (PHILLIPS). The Greek word for "turned" means she changed her course of action, not merely the direction she was facing.[13] Not only her view but also her life changed in an instant.

He is risen! He is risen indeed!

. . . and [she] cried out in Aramaic, "Rabboni!" . . . *John 20:16*

We hear your joy, Mary, resounding across the centuries. "Master!" (WE). "Teacher!" (NLV). To have watched Him die and then to see Him alive. To witness His burial and then to experience His resurrection. No wonder Mary Magdalene reached out to touch Him.

Jesus said, "Do not hold on to me, . . ." *John 20:17*

Oh dear. That's not what any of us were expecting, least of all Mary. Though the words sound harsh—"Do not cling to me" (ESV), "Touch me not" (GNV)—surely Jesus spoke them with great tenderness. He wasn't chastising Mary; He was helping her let go.

Whether she'd taken His hand or grasped the hem of His robe, either from an overflow of affection or pure adoration, Jesus could not tarry in the garden with her a moment longer.

". . . for I have not yet ascended to the Father." *John 20:17*

In forty days He would "go up, ascend, arise."[14] Imagine how eager He must have been! "I haven't yet gone up to my Father" (CEB), He told her. Though Jesus had His eyes fixed on heaven, He still had time for Mary Magdalene.

I just have to say that again. Jesus *paused to speak to a woman.* Not merely to speak to her but to *send* her. Weeks later Jesus would proclaim the Great Commission[15] when He sent the Eleven into the world to preach the gospel. But first He sent Mary Magdalene to share the truth with *them.*

Can a woman spread the good news? Oh yes she can!

> "Go instead to my brothers and tell them, . . ." *John 20:17*

He commanded her to go, even though Mary and her sisters had already gone to the disciples earlier that morning, had told them about the resurrection, and were written off as madwomen. God doesn't call us to go once, and then we're done. He calls us to keep going until the work is finished. "Go to those who believe in me" (NIrV), Jesus said.

The Lord had a different truth for Mary to proclaim this time. Not simply that He was risen—amazing as that was—but that He would soon rise straight into His Father's arms.

> ". . . 'I am ascending to my Father and your Father, to my God and your God.'" *John 20:17*

I love the original Greek—"God of me, and God of you."[16] A reminder they were *family,* this small but mighty group of believers, and they would all be in heaven together someday.

Commissioned by the Lord Himself, entrusted with the most important announcement in history, did Mary Magdalene balk? Argue? Insist He come with her? She did not. Like the prophet Isaiah, Mary declared, if only with her actions, "Here am I. Send me!"[17]

> Mary Magdalene went to the disciples with the news: . . . *John 20:18*

Did she run? That's my vote. "Away came Mary Magdalene" (AMPC), as fast as her sandal-covered feet could take her until she "found the disciples" (NLT).

Jesus had given her a simple message to relay. The same simple message He gives us. *Tell the world I am alive. Tell the world I am your God.* Can you do it, sister? Say to a stranger, "I serve a risen Savior, who loves His own"? Confess to a coworker, "I believe in Jesus, who died for my sins and lives in my heart"?

Mary Magdalene shows us the way. With Christ's authority she "announced" (CEB), "informed" (NET), and began joyfully "reporting to the disciples" (AMP) the living proof they'd been waiting to hear.

> . . . "I have seen the Lord!" *John 20:18*

Oh, those five world-shaking words!

Her expression, her exuberance, her exaltation made it abundantly clear that she had not seen Him lying in the grave. "I saw the Lord!" (EXB), she told them. She'd heard Him speak her name, she'd touched Him for an instant, and she'd definitely seen Him fully alive.

This is where I start thinking, *If only I'd lived in the time of Jesus. If only I'd seen Him with my own eyes.* Then I remind myself we can see the Lord *every day.* Shining forth from the pages of His Word. Reflected in the faces of those who are filled with His Spirit. Captured in the moments of true worship spoken and sung in our churches.

He is more alive than ever, my friend, and He is coming back!

Job, who lived after the Flood and long before Moses, said "I know that my redeemer lives, and that in the end he will stand on the earth."[18] Some two thousand years later, Mary Magdalene—*a woman*—echoed the same amazing revelation.

> And she told them that he had said these things to her.
> *John 20:18*

Mary accurately reported "what Jesus had said to her" (EXB). Did the disciples leap to their feet and shout with joy? Or did they remain unconvinced and wonder if Mary Magdalene was flirting with madness again?

Here's what happened that Easter afternoon.

> Now that same day two of them were going to a village called Emmaus, about seven miles from Jerusalem. *Luke 24:13*

Two of His faithful followers were traveling on foot and talking about everything that had happened. When Jesus Himself walked up, "they were kept from recognizing him"[19] and with downcast faces told Him about Jesus of Nazareth, who was "powerful in word and deed before God and all the people."[20] The two described His arrest and crucifixion and confessed, "We had hoped that he was the one who was going to redeem Israel."[21]

We're shaking our heads, thinking, *What about Mary Magdalene? What about the women? What about their reports?*

The two heard, but they did not understand. They remembered, but they did not believe. And they admitted as much to this stranger by their side.

> "In addition, some of our women amazed us." *Luke 24:22*

Amazed sounds as if the news was received positively, but we know better. Closer to the mark? "Our womenfolk have disturbed us profoundly" (PHILLIPS) and "completely confused us" (MSG) and "made us afeared" (WYC)—my personal favorite. The Greek literally means they were "beside themselves."[22]

The two continued, apparently eager to share what their womenfolk did.

> "They went to the tomb early this morning but didn't find his body." *Luke 24:22–23*

Again, their account was accurate. Then disbelief crept into the disciples' words.

> "They came and told us that they had seen a vision of angels, who said he was alive." *Luke 24:23*

Mary Magdalene and the team didn't have a *vision* of angels. They *saw* angels. Theirs was not a "special dream" (NLV) or an "apparition of messengers" (YLT). The angels were real—as alive as Jesus Himself—yet most of His followers seemed uncertain of their appearance or their message. Maybe that's why they still questioned the truth of the resurrection.

> "Then some of our companions went to the tomb and found it just as the women had said, but they did not see Jesus." *Luke 24:24*

True, Peter and John did race to the tomb, but "him they saw not" (YLT). We imagine these two on the road to Emmaus struggling to believe, still convinced this was some crazy story the women had made up.

Jesus quickly put an end to such thinking.

> He said to them, "How foolish you are, and how slow to believe all that the prophets have spoken!" *Luke 24:25*

Starting with Moses, Jesus explained all the scriptures that talked about Him. Even so, these two couldn't see the truth literally before their eyes. Not until they talked Jesus into joining them for dinner and He broke bread "and began to give it to them. Then their eyes were opened and they recognized him, and he disappeared from their sight."[23]

These two people had an encounter with Christ on the road to Emmaus. My first encounter with Him was on the road to Nowhere. Not only was I not headed His way, but I was running in the opposite direction.

Nonetheless, Jesus knew how to get my attention. Two new

believers crossed my path one autumn day. They took me as I was and loved me into the kingdom. They said, "Look at His words! Look at His story!" When I opened the Bible, He was there on every page.

Two thousand years ago that's what Jesus told His disciples to do: *"Look!"*

On Easter night He appeared to the Eleven and said, "Why do doubts rise in your minds? Look at my hands and my feet. It is I myself!"[24] Then He "opened their minds so they could understand the Scriptures."[25] This is how much the Lord loves His people. Despite our doubts and fears, He continues to open our minds and hearts and teach us His truth.

Something else miraculous happened on that sacred day in Jerusalem. Since it's in God's Word, we know it's real, but it's still mind boggling.

> The bodies of many holy people who had died were raised to life. *Matthew 27:52*

"Many godly men and women" (TLB) were resurrected. Not a few. A lot. These were the "bodies of the saints" (DRA) who had "fallen asleep" (ESV), the same phrase the Lord had used about Lazarus. And these dead people, en masse, "were made to stand up alive" (OJB) on Easter morning.[26] *Seriously?* Yes, indeed.

> They came out of the tombs after Jesus' resurrection . . .
> *Matthew 27:53*

Jesus came out first and foremost. His resurrection is the one that matters, the one that makes all other resurrections possible.

On Easter morning we don't proclaim, "*They* are risen!" We shout, "*He* is risen!"

Still, this was a mighty display of His power. "After Jesus had risen to life, they came out of their graves" (CEV) and "left the cemetery" (NLT). Are you picturing this?

> . . . and went into the holy city and appeared to many people. *Matthew 27:53*

What better way for the Lord to affirm His victory over death than to send out other resurrected people to spread the news—"to exhibit, to appear (in person), to declare."[27] If a formerly dead person walked past me on the street, alive and breathing, she wouldn't need to say or do *one thing* for me to be fully convinced that resurrection was possible!

Even so, our curious human nature often wants to know more than what's given us in Scripture. How many saints rose from the dead? Did they have human bodies or glorified bodies? Who saw them? How long did they stay in Jerusalem? When did they disappear, and where did they go?

Three centuries ago commentator Matthew Henry wisely wrote, "These are secret things which belong not to us."[28] Such mysteries are the Lord's alone. Even wise King Solomon cautioned that we'll "never be able to understand what God is doing. However hard you try, you will never find out. The wise may claim to know, but they don't."[29]

It's true. The scholarly books I researched didn't provide any definitive answers about the resurrected saints who appeared in Jerusalem. For me, it's enough to know it happened. After all, Easter was filled with singular events.

Jesus raised these holy people from the dead so they could be His witnesses on earth. How much more are we, the living church, called to appear before the people of our own cities and proclaim His resurrection!

After "many convincing proofs" during "a period of forty days,"[30] Jesus led His disciples "out to the vicinity of Bethany."[31] We don't hear from Mary and Martha in this scene, but the sisters surely would not have missed this sacred moment so close to home. Even if they stood some distance away, like the women at the cross after Jesus died, I believe with all my heart that Mary of Bethany and her sister were present.

The Lord's last recorded words offered hope for the future. How like Jesus to let His followers know good things were coming. He told them, "In a few days you will be baptized with the Holy Spirit."[32] Then He was "taken up before their very eyes, and a cloud hid him from their sight."[33]

At last the Son would be reunited with His Father.

> They were looking intently up into the sky as he was going, when suddenly two men dressed in white stood beside them. *Acts 1:10*

Might they be the same two angels Mary Magdalene saw at the tomb? In any case, they fit the description, which meant the male disciples could more easily accept the women's testimonies, having now seen angels for themselves.

It has never been the Lord's intent to divide men and women in the body of Christ. We may experience Him in different ways and come to understand His truths through various methods, but we're all His body, meant to function as one. "There is one body and one Spirit, just as you were called to one hope when you were called; one Lord, one faith, one baptism; one God and Father of all, who is over all and through all and in all."[34]

Throughout these extraordinary scenes from Scripture, we've watched Jesus bridge the gap between His male disciples and His female followers. When the men returned to Jerusalem after Jesus's resurrection and "went upstairs to the room where they were staying,"[35] they were not alone—at least not for long.

In this upper room "they all joined together constantly in prayer, along with the women and Mary the mother of Jesus."[36] *Yes!* The women were there, and Mary of Nazareth in particular. Once considered the mother of a great teacher, Mary would forever be identified as the mother of the Son of God, who defeated death and rose from the grave.

Though neither Mary of Bethany nor Mary Magdalene is named here, I am content to know that women were present. I can see our women of Easter there. Praying with their heads bowed and their hearts open. Waiting for the Holy Spirit to make His appearance, even as they'd waited for their Holy Savior.

He came as an infant. He will come again as an invincible warrior. For now, not only at Easter but in every season of the year, the Lord's calling is clear: "Go, tell."[37]

So, let's go, beloved. Let's *go* and let's *tell*. Like our little girl in yellow, jumping up and down for Jesus, we're called to be joyful, hopeful, faithful. The world is looking for answers, and because of Jesus, we have them. Now He wants us to share them.

You and I can be Easter women every day of the year, living in the freedom of His resurrection and singing out with all our hearts, "He lives! He lives!"

Christ the Lord is risen today, Alleluia!
Earth and heaven in chorus say, Alleluia!
Raise your joys and triumphs high, Alleluia!
Sing, ye heavens, and earth reply, Alleluia!

Love's redeeming work is done, Alleluia!
Fought the fight, the battle won, Alleluia!
Death in vain forbids him rise, Alleluia!
Christ has opened paradise, Alleluia!

Lives again our glorious King, Alleluia!
Where, O death, is now thy sting? Alleluia!
Once he died our souls to save, Alleluia!
Where's thy victory, boasting grave? Alleluia!

Soar we now where Christ has led, Alleluia!
Following our exalted Head, Alleluia!
Made like him, like him we rise, Alleluia!
Ours the cross, the grave, the skies, Alleluia!

—CHARLES WESLEY, "CHRIST THE LORD IS RISEN TODAY," 1739

Study Guide

Are you ready to go deeper? To look more intently at the lives of our three Marys and the One they loved? This study guide was designed with you in mind, whether you're exploring on your own or in a small-group setting.

It's been wisely said, "We are closer to God when we are asking questions than when we think we have the answers."[1] Our goal here is to study His Word and learn from Him. We'll examine our faith through the lens of these biblical scenes and wait expectantly for God's wisdom and direction.

Included in this guide you'll find quotes from several contemporary women who shared their heartfelt comments through my online Bible study. Their words serve as a reminder of the vast community of faith, both modern and ancient, of which we are each a part, and of the rich insights we can gain from our sisters.

> *"Jesus uses women in His kingdom in mighty ways, in intimate ways, in loving ways."*
>
> —AMY

You'll need a place to write your thoughts—a notebook, journal, tablet, or whatever works best for you—and the willingness to open both your Bible and your heart. Choose a reading plan that suits your busy schedule. You might begin *The Women of Easter* early in the year and study one chapter a week throughout the Lenten season, answering the study-guide questions as you go. Or you could read two chapters each Sunday in the month leading up to Easter. Or you could immerse yourself in one chapter a day during Holy Week, beginning on Palm Sunday.

However you approach it, I pray you'll have a new view of Easter after spending time with Mary of Bethany, Mary of Nazareth, and Mary Magdalene. May those discoveries remain with you long after you've proclaimed, "He is risen!"

Chapter One: Lost in His Love

Read Luke 10:38–42 and John 11:1–15.

1. The high-profile presence of Mary of Bethany and her older sister, Martha, in the gospel narrative affirms a "high role for women's faith."[2] Even so, the Lord chastened Martha for being "worried and upset"[3] as He commended Mary for having "chosen what is better."[4] What did you learn from watching busy Martha and quiet Mary? In what sense were their differences a matter of personality? And in what sense were those distinctions spiritual? Why do you think He praised one sister's approach over the other?

2. A thousand years before Mary of Bethany was born, King David wrote, "One thing have I desired of the LORD, that will I seek after; that I may dwell in the house of the LORD all the days of my life, to behold the beauty of the LORD, and to enquire in his temple."[5] What is the "one thing" you desire most from the Lord?

Practically speaking, how can you dwell in God's house, as King David described, and yet go about your day-to-day life? What further insight do you find in these words from Brother Lawrence: "The soul's eyes must be kept on God, particularly when something is being done in the outside world"[6]?

3. We know that "Jesus loved Martha and her sister and Lazarus,"[7] yet He allowed each of them to suffer, if only for a handful of days. What does 1 Peter 1:6–7 suggest to you about God's purposes for pain in our lives? "For a little while you may have had to suffer grief in all kinds of trials. These have come so that the proven genuineness of your faith—of greater worth than gold, which perishes even though refined by fire—may result in praise, glory and honor when Jesus Christ is revealed." What trial have you withstood that tested and refined your faith? In what ways did you sense God's purpose in it all?

Chapter Two: Mary Went to Meet the Lord

Read John 11:17–53.

1. By the time Martha next spoke with Jesus, her faith had taken a leap forward. She told the Lord, "I believe that you are the Messiah, the Son of God."[8] How does her declaration change—or reinforce—your view of Martha? In the same way, when Jesus asked his disciples, "Who do you say I am?"[9] Simon Peter was quick to

answer, "You are the Messiah, the Son of the living God."[10] Jesus told Peter, "This was not revealed to you by flesh and blood, but by my Father in heaven."[11] What might Jesus's response to Peter indicate about Martha's relationship with her heavenly Father? When and where have you felt prompted to confess that Jesus is the Son of God? And why?

2. Both Martha and Mary said in turn, "Lord, if you had been here, my brother would not have died."[12] Think of a time when you felt that God's response to your need came too late and you wondered if He truly cared. What did you express to Him in your prayers? How did His apparent delay impact your faith? We aren't told how Mary or Martha felt, but the Lord's emotions are described in detail. He was "deeply moved in spirit and troubled"[13] until at last "Jesus wept."[14] How does the image of Him weeping affect your view of Him and your faith in Him?

3. Jesus accomplished several things when He raised Lazarus from the dead. See how many positive outcomes you can list beyond the obvious: a new life for Mary and Martha's brother. In what specific ways did the resurrection of Lazarus prepare hearts for the Lord's resurrection to come? What do these words of Jesus—"I am the resurrection and the life"[15]—suggest about His power to restore a shattered dream or resurrect a dying relationship and make things right again?

Chapter Three: I Still Would Choose the Better Part

Read John 11:54–12:8 and Mark 14:3–9.

1. The Lord waited in Ephraim with His followers, knowing the agony ahead in Jerusalem. Psalm 27:14 tells us, "Wait for the LORD; be strong and take heart and wait for the LORD." If you are going through a difficult period of waiting right now, what can you do to strengthen your heart? How could other believers encourage you? And how could you encourage another believer who is going through a painful time of waiting?

2. Mary of Bethany helped prepare Jesus for the suffering to come by humbly pouring out her love for Him in a fragrant and tangible expression of worship. If you assume certain physical positions during worship— bowing your head, folding your hands, kneeling, lying prostrate on the floor—how do those actions impact you in the moment? Are you more likely to do them publicly in church or privately at home, and why? What does it mean to you to sit at the Lord's feet, spiritually speaking?

"My most profound moments of worship take place when no one is watching, which makes Mary's very public moment with her Savior all the more courageous."

—NICOLE

3. Jesus personally commended four individuals[16] in Scripture: John the Baptist,[17] a Roman centurion,[18] a Canaanite woman,[19] and Mary of Bethany.[20] Note that two of the four people were women. What significance do you find in each of His choices? He said of Mary, "With what she had she did all she could."[21] What could you sacrifice as an act of worship to Jesus? What would it take for you to offer such an extravagant gift to the Lord?

"Though Martha and Mary both loved Jesus, it is Mary of Bethany we remember as truly worshiping Him."

—Janice

Chapter Four: With Palms Before Thee

Read John 12:9–19, Luke 19:37–42, and Matthew 21:1–17.

1. On the first Palm Sunday, the crowd loudly praised God for all the miracles they had seen.[22] How does your church observe Palm Sunday? And how do you celebrate that day in your heart? What prompts you to praise God any day of the year? His goodness? His faithfulness? His love? Make a list of His divine qualities that would inspire you to shout "Blessed is he who comes in the name of the Lord!"[23]

2. On the heels of His triumphant entrance into Jerusalem, the Lord was confronted with moneychangers in

the temple courts—a jarring reminder of mankind's disregard for the sacred and its endless obsession with money. The Lord could have ordered His disciples to overturn the tables. Why was it important for Jesus to do this Himself? What message might His actions have communicated to those who were watching? And how does this scene speak to you personally?

3. Moments later we find Jesus healing the blind and the lame. How do you reconcile these juxtaposed images of Him angrily tossing aside a table one minute and then gently healing people the next? In the same way, how might you explain "God is a righteous judge, a God who displays his wrath every day"[24] in light of the promise that "his compassions never fail. They are new every morning"?[25] As you form your answers, imagine you are sitting across from a friend who has not yet confessed Christ as her Savior and is trying to understand how a God of wrath can also be a God of love. What would you say to her?

Chapter Five: O Most Afflicted!

Read Luke 20:1–8, Luke 21:1–4, Luke 22:3–13, John 13:3–10, and Matthew 26:20–56.

1. When you read the story of the widow with two mites, do you identify more with the wealthy people who gave relatively little or the woman with little who gave all she had? Explain your answer. In 2 Corinthians 9:7 we're

told, "Each of you should give what you have decided in your heart to give, not reluctantly or under compulsion, for God loves a cheerful giver." What "cheer" do you find in the widow's sacrifice? Why do you think giving cheerfully matters to God? And what parallels do you find between the way the widow gave and the way Jesus was about to give His life?

2. In this chapter I related a story about a time I side-stepped the truth regarding my writing ministry, and then I concluded, "What we *think* we'll do when our faith is put to the test and what we *actually* do are often two different things." Describe a situation in which you deliberately avoided mentioning your relationship with Christ. Is that the same as denying Him? Why or why not? What did you learn from your experience?

3. Throughout the Last Supper, it's apparent that Jesus's closest friends were unaware of the dark hours ahead. Yet He did not chastise them for their ignorance. He simply told them, "Later you will understand."[26] In the garden at Gethsemane, when the disciples who were supposed to pray for Him fell asleep, not once but three times, Jesus didn't punish them. He only asked, "Are you still sleeping and resting?"[27] What do the Lord's reactions here, and His reactions to Peter's denial as well, tell us about His relationship with His followers? What comfort does that offer you when you fear you've failed Him?

Chapter Six: Thorns Thine Only Crown

Read Luke 2:34–35, Mark 14:55–65, Matthew 26:69–75, and Luke 23:1–43.

1. The physical abuse endured by Jesus began long before He reached Golgotha: spitting, striking, flogging, dragging, piercing. In the chapter I asked, "Could you bear to watch?" When I posed that question to my blog readers, their responses were divided:

"I would have been there. Not to suffer alongside my Lord? How would I ever be able to reconcile that?"

—DEB

"I would be in the vicinity, perhaps ministering to others. But I could not watch His torture."

—BONNIE

How about you, friend? Could you have remained by His side through it all? Perhaps Jesus is asking you to do something right now that you think is beyond your ability—or willingness—to endure. How could you muster the courage to stand, as our women of Easter did?

2. Women were definitely present as He staggered toward the cross. Though they "mourned and wailed for him,"[28] Jesus urged them to weep for themselves and for their children, "with an eye to the destruction that was coming

upon Jerusalem."[29] What does this brief exchange tell you about the women? And, even more, about Jesus?

"We aren't just women in His eyes; we are His daughters, and He loves us deeply."

— CHARLOTTE

3. Having read the crucifixion accounts in this chapter and in the scriptures listed above, now open your Bible to Psalm 22, written by King David, an earthly ancestor of King Jesus. Take note of the dozen or so verses that parallel the biblical description of the crucifixion, from the opening line of the psalm, "My God, my God, why have you forsaken me?"[30] to the heartfelt plea "You are my strength; come quickly to help me."[31] What strikes you as you read David's ancient lyrics? Compare them to the crucifixion itself. How does the fulfilling of these many prophecies impact your faith in God and in His Word?

Chapter Seven: At the Cross Her Station Keeping

Read John 19:25–27, Matthew 27:45–56, John 19:28–41, Luke 23:55–56, and Mark 16:1.

1. Our sorrow deepens when we return to the book of John: "Near the cross of Jesus stood his mother."[32] Mary of Nazareth was not only present; she was close. Close enough to see Him, to touch Him, to catch the scent of His blood and sweat, to hear Him groan in agony.

"I've wondered if Mary's friends and family told her not to go—not only for her own safety, but also to spare her from seeing such violence, brutality, and suffering."

—BURQAJ

Despite whoever might have objected, Mary was at the cross. While the others watched their friend, their teacher, their Savior die, Mary watched her son die. If you were Mary's sister, standing next to her, what words of comfort would you have offered? Or might you have remained silent? What truth or hope do you think Mary clung to in that desperate hour?

2. In this chapter we see the start of what are traditionally called the Seven Last Words of Christ:

    1. "Father, forgive them, for they do not know what they are doing." *Luke 23:34*
    2. "Truly I tell you, today you will be with me in paradise." *Luke 23:43*
    3. "Woman, here is your son," and to the disciple, "Here is your mother." *John 19:26–27*
    4. *"Eli, Eli, lema sabachthani?"* (which means "My God, my God, why have you forsaken me?"). *Matthew 27:46*
    5. "I am thirsty." *John 19:28*
    6. "It is finished." *John 19:30*
    7. "Father, into your hands I commit my spirit." *Luke 23:46*

Choose one of the seven statements that's especially powerful to you, and describe whom Jesus was addressing, what His statement or question meant at the moment, and what it reveals about His character. What difference does that final word from Jesus make in your life today?

3. When He breathed His last, the women were still there. When His body was taken down from the cross, the women were still there. And when His body was laid in a tomb, Mary Magdalene and another Mary were still there. What significance might there be regarding the presence of the women and the apparent absence of the men? Might Jesus have been honoring the women? Protecting the disciples? Why do you think the women remained by His side to the very end?

"The strength, dedication, love, and faithfulness these women showed to our Lord astounds me. I want that kind of heart."
— DANA

Chapter Eight: I Know That My Redeemer Lives

Read Mark 16:2–8, Luke 24:9–11, John 20:11–18, Luke 24:13–53, and Acts 1:3–14.

1. The first Easter. After so much sorrow came so much joy. And our sisters led the parade. What does the prominence of women in the life, death, and resurrec-

tion of Jesus mean to you? In what ways does their faithfulness challenge you to deepen your relationship with God? Write down the next important step you need to take in your walk of faith and how and when you're going to take it.

2. One commentator called Mary Magdalene's encounter with Jesus at the garden tomb "the most humanly moving of all the stories of the risen Christ."[33] As you read through it here, pay attention to Mary Magdalene's emotional journey, captured in her words and actions:

> He asked her, "Woman, why are you crying? Who is it you are looking for?"
>
> Thinking he was the gardener, she said, "Sir, if you have carried him away, tell me where you have put him, and I will get him."
>
> Jesus said to her, "Mary."
>
> She turned toward him and cried out in Aramaic, "Rabboni!" (which means "Teacher").
>
> Jesus said, "Do not hold on to me, for I have not yet ascended to the Father. Go instead to my brothers and tell them, 'I am ascending to my Father and your Father, to my God and your God.'"
>
> Mary Magdalene went to the disciples with the news: "I have seen the Lord!" *John 20:15–18*

Just as Jesus moved from death to life, so was Mary's faith resurrected. Are you ready to share your faith with

others? Where do you need to go and whom do you
need to tell?

*"As the celebration of Easter approaches, I feel deeply
convicted to witness to others—more strongly than at any
other time during the year."*

—TIFFANY

3. Now that you've met the women of Easter, which of our
    three Marys has taught you the most by example? Mary
    of Bethany, with her teachable heart, quiet humility,
    and breathtaking generosity? Mary of Nazareth, with
    her steadfast support, unflagging faith, and boundless
    courage? Or Mary Magdalene, with her deep commit-
    ment, her willingness to both lead and follow, and a
    boldness born of the Spirit? If you have a favorite Mary,
    explain what you learned from her and how you could
    follow in her footsteps.

God bless you for opening God's Word with me this sacred season. Happy Easter, my sister. He is risen indeed!

Notes

A Season of Grace
1. Isaiah 53:3, KJV
2. Matthew 4:2

Chapter 1: Lost in His Love
1. Robert L. Thomas, ed., *New American Standard Exhaustive Concordance of the Bible with Hebrew-Aramaic and Greek Dictionaries* (Nashville: Holman, 1981), 1636.
2. Matthew Henry, *Matthew Henry's Commentary on the Whole Bible* (Peabody, MA: Hendrickson, 1991), 5:842.
3. Alexander Moody Stuart, *The Three Marys: Mary of Magdala, Mary of Bethany, Mary of Nazareth* (Edinburgh, Scotland: Banner of Truth, 1984), 157.
4. Stuart, *The Three Marys,* 147.
5. Edith Deen, *All the Women of the Bible* (New York: Harper and Row, 1955), 177.
6. Lindsay Hardin Freeman, *Bible Women: All Their Words and Why They Matter* (Cincinnati: Forward Movement, 2014), 427.
7. Rose Sallberg Kam, *Their Stories, Our Stories: Women of the Bible* (New York: Continuum, 1995), 219.
8. Stuart, *The Three Marys,* 152.
9. 1 Peter 4:9
10. Dolores Kimball, *Memorial: The Mystery of Mary of Bethany* (Darlington, UK: EP Books, 2014), 66.
11. Virginia Stem Owens, *Daughters of Eve: Women of the Bible Speak to Women of Today* (Colorado Springs: NavPress, 1995), 146.
12. Thomas, *New American Standard Concordance,* 1664.

13. John 1:1
14. Acts 22:3, AMPC
15. Matthew 11:29
16. Kimball, *Memorial,* 21.
17. Synagogue.cz, www.synagogue.cz/the-old-new-synagogue-page /about-the-synagogue/.
18. Kam, *Their Stories, Our Stories,* 219.
19. Thomas, *New American Standard Concordance,* 1675.
20. Thomas, *New American Standard Concordance,* 1659.
21. Frances Vander Velde, *Women of the Bible* (Grand Rapids: Kregel, 1985), 175.
22. Miriam Feinberg Vamosh, *Women at the Time of the Bible* (Herzlia, Israel: Palphot, 2007), 20.
23. Kimball, *Memorial,* 24.
24. Stuart, *The Three Marys,* 159.
25. Kimball, *Memorial,* 22.
26. John 6:27
27. Stuart, *The Three Marys,* 169.
28. Martha Kilpatrick, *Adoration: Mary of Bethany—The Untold Story* (Suches, GA: Shulamite Ministries, 1999), 22.
29. Stuart, *The Three Marys,* 159.
30. Psalm 16:5
31. Kimball, *Memorial,* 29.
32. Ephesians 4:23–24
33. H. V. Morton, *Women of the Bible* (New York: Dodd, Mead, 1941), 164.
34. Joyce Hollyday, *Clothed with the Sun: Biblical Women, Social Justice and Us* (Louisville, KY: Westminster John Knox, 1994), 227.
35. Thomas, *New American Standard Concordance,* 1691.
36. Frederick Dale Bruner, *The Gospel of John: A Commentary* (Grand Rapids: Eerdmans, 2012), 659.
37. John 10:40
38. Bruner, *The Gospel of John,* 656.
39. 2 Corinthians 4:17
40. Bruner, *The Gospel of John,* 660.
41. Thomas, *New American Standard Concordance,* 1628.

42. Thomas, *New American Standard Concordance,* 1627.

43. Stuart, *The Three Marys,* 156.

44. Henry, *Matthew Henry's Commentary,* 5:843.

45. Miriam Feinberg Vamosh, *Daily Life at the Time of Jesus* (Herzlia, Israel: Palphot, 2007), 72.

46. Thomas, *New American Standard Concordance,* 1628.

47. Thomas, *New American Standard Concordance,* 1650.

48. 1 Thessalonians 4:13

49. Psalm 145:13

Chapter 2: Mary Went to Meet the Lord

1. Rose Sallberg Kam, *Their Stories, Our Stories: Women of the Bible* (New York: Continuum, 1995), 219.

2. *The Expanded Bible: Explore the Depths of the Scriptures While You Read* (Nashville: Nelson, 2011), note on John 11:17.

3. Matthew Henry, *Matthew Henry's Commentary on the Whole Bible* (Peabody, MA: Hendrickson, 1991), 5:846.

4. Robert L. Thomas, ed., *New American Standard Exhaustive Concordance of the Bible with Hebrew-Aramaic and Greek Dictionaries* (Nashville: Holman, 1981), *para* 1672 + *muthos* 1667.

5. Eli Lizorkin-Eyzenberg, *The Jewish Gospel of John: Discovering Jesus, King of All Israel* (Tel Aviv, Israel: Jewish Studies for Christians, 2015), 188.

6. Donald Guthrie, "John," in *The New Bible Commentary Revised,* ed. Donald Guthrie (Grand Rapids: Eerdmans, 1970), 953.

7. Thomas, *New American Standard Concordance,* 1657.

8. Thomas, *New American Standard Concordance,* 1601.

9. Dolores Kimball, *Memorial: The Mystery of Mary of Bethany* (Darlington, UK: EP Books, 2014), 22.

10. Guthrie, "John," 953.

11. Lizorkin-Eyzenberg, *The Jewish Gospel of John,* 186.

12. Kimball, *Memorial,* 61.

13. 1 Corinthians 6:14

14. Henry, *Matthew Henry's Commentary,* 5:842–43.

15. 1 Peter 1:9

16. Lizorkin-Eyzenberg, *The Jewish Gospel of John*, 186.
17. Thomas, *New American Standard Concordance*, 1663.
18. Kimball, *Memorial*, 95.
19. Thomas, *New American Standard Concordance*, 1648.
20. Henry, *Matthew Henry's Commentary*, 5:850.
21. Martha Kilpatrick, *Adoration: Mary of Bethany—The Untold Story* (Suches, GA: Shulamite Ministries, 1999), 72.
22. Matthew 6:10, KJV
23. Julie-Allyson Ieron, *Names of Women of the Bible* (Chicago: Moody, 1998), 156.
24. Romans 12:15, NASB
25. George Matheson, *The Representative Women of the Bible* (London: Hodder and Stoughton, 1908), 276.
26. Thomas, *New American Standard Concordance*, 1648.
27. Thomas, *New American Standard Concordance*, 1670.
28. Frederick Dale Bruner, *The Gospel of John: A Commentary* (Grand Rapids: Eerdmans, 2012), 679.
29. John 11:26
30. Henry, *Matthew Henry's Commentary*, 5:853.
31. Luke 7:11–15
32. Luke 8:41–42, 49–55
33. Bruner, *The Gospel of John*, 685.
34. Psalm 73:7
35. John 11:48

Chapter 3: I Still Would Choose the Better Part

1. Luke 9:44–45
2. Luke 8:1–2
3. Luke 8:3
4. R. Kiefer, "John," in *Oxford Bible Commentary*, ed. John Barton and John Muddiman (New York: Oxford University Press, 2001), 983.
5. Miriam Feinberg Vamosh, *Women at the Time of the Bible* (Herzlia, Israel: Palphot, 2008), 30.
6. Simon Sebag Montefiore, *Jerusalem: The Biography* (New York: Knopf, 2011), 106.

7. Dolores Kimball, *Memorial: The Mystery of Mary of Bethany* (Darlington, UK: EP Books, 2014), 9.

8. Hebrews 12:2

9. "Saturday of the Holy and Righteous Friend of Christ, Lazarus," Greek Orthodox Archdiocese of America, Great Lent, Holy Week and Pascha in the Eastern Orthodox Christian Church, http://lent.goarch.org/saturday_of_lazarus/learn/.

10. Rose Sallberg Kam, *Their Stories, Our Stories: Women of the Bible* (New York: Continuum, 1995), 222–23.

11. Robert L. Thomas, ed., *New American Standard Exhaustive Concordance of the Bible with Hebrew-Aramaic and Greek Dictionaries* (Nashville: Holman, 1981), 1588.

12. Alexander Moody Stuart, *The Three Marys: Mary of Magdala, Mary of Bethany, Mary of Nazareth* (Edinburgh, Scotland: Banner of Truth, 1984), 190.

13. D. A. Carson, "Matthew," in *The Expositor's Bible Commentary,* ed. Frank E. Gaebelein (Grand Rapids, Zondervan, 1984), 8:526.

14. James 2:25

15. Stuart, *The Three Marys,* 184.

16. Frederick Dale Bruner, *The Gospel of John: A Commentary* (Grand Rapids: Eerdmans, 2012), 704.

17. Luke 7:37, CEV

18. Kimball, *Memorial,* 7.

19. Kimball, *Memorial,* 7.

20. Eli Lizorkin-Eyzenberg, *The Jewish Gospel of John: Discovering Jesus, King of All Israel* (Tel Aviv, Israel: Jewish Studies for Christians, 2015), 198.

21. J. C. Trever, "Nard," in *The Interpreter's Dictionary of the Bible: An Illustrated Encyclopedia,* ed. George Arthur Buttrick (Nashville: Abingdon, 1962), 3:510.

22. Carson, "Matthew," 8:526.

23. Mark 14:3, TLB

24. *The Expanded Bible: Explore the Depths of the Scriptures While You Read* (Nashville: Thomas Nelson, 2011), note on John 12:3.

25. James Faulkner, *Romances and Intrigues of the Women of the Bible* (New York: Vantage, 1957), 129.

26. Matthew 26:7

27. Donald Guthrie, "John," in *The New Bible Commentary Revised*, ed. Donald Guthrie (Grand Rapids: Eerdmans, 1970), 955.

28. Luke 10:39

29. John 11:32–33

30. Stuart, *The Three Marys*, 192.

31. John 12:3, Bible Hub, http://biblehub.com/text/john/12-3.htm.

32. 1 Corinthians 11:15

33. Lizorkin-Eyzenberg, *The Jewish Gospel of John*, 198.

34. Martha Kilpatrick, *Adoration: Mary of Bethany—The Untold Story* (Suches, GA: Shulamite Ministries, 1999), 8.

35. Guthrie, "John," 955.

36. Carolyn Nabors Baker, *Caught in a Higher Love: Inspiring Stories of Women in the Bible* (Nashville: Broadman and Holman, 1998), 80.

37. Lindsay Hardin Freeman, *Bible Women: All Their Words and Why They Matter* (Cincinnati: Forward Movement, 2014), 428.

38. Matthew Henry, *Matthew Henry's Commentary on the Whole Bible* (Peabody, MA: Hendrickson, 1991), 5:862.

39. PayScale, www.payscale.com/research/US/Job=Laborer/Hourly_Rate.

40. Mark 8:36, NLT

41. Guthrie, "John," 955.

42. Matthew 26:8

43. Walter W. Wessel, "Mark," in *The Expositor's Bible Commentary*, ed. Frank E. Gaebelein (Grand Rapids: Zondervan, 1992), 8:756.

44. George Matheson, *The Representative Women of the Bible* (London: Hodder and Stoughton, 1908), 264.

45. Mark 16:1

46. Stuart, *The Three Marys*, 193.

47. Mark 8:31

48. Mark 8:32
49. Stuart, *The Three Marys,* 194.
50. Lizorkin-Eyzenberg, *The Jewish Gospel of John,* 199.
51. Stuart, *The Three Marys,* 199.
52. Matthew 24:14, NET
53. Edith Deen, *All the Women of the Bible* (New York: Harper and Row, 1955), 176.

Chapter 4: With Palms Before Thee

1. Isaiah 49:16, NASB
2. Leviticus 23:40
3. Acts 4:26
4. Matthew 9:10–13
5. John 12:12
6. Ernest L. Martin, "The Significance of Bethphage on the Mount of Olives," Hope of Israel Ministries (Ecclesia of Yehovah), www.hope-of-israel.org/bethpage.html.
7. Luke 8:2–3
8. James Faulkner, *Romances and Intrigues of the Women of the Bible* (New York: Vantage, 1957), 130.
9. D. A. Carson, "Matthew," in *The Expositor's Bible Commentary,* ed. Frank E. Gaebelein (Grand Rapids: Zondervan, 1992), 8:437.
10. Luke 19:30
11. Matthew 5:18, NASB
12. Zechariah 9:9
13. John 12:15, EXB
14. 1 Kings 1:32–34
15. "Appreciating the Role of Mules and Donkeys on the Farm," Mother Earth News, December 2002/January 2003, www.motherearthnews.com/homesteading-and-livestock/mules-and-donkeys-on-the-farm-zmaz02djzgoe.aspx.
16. John 12:15, TLB
17. Proverbs 3:6
18. John 12:14, VOICE
19. Matthew 21:9

20. John 12:13
21. John 12:13, EXB
22. Psalm 118:26
23. 1 Kings 1:39
24. 1 Kings 1:40
25. 1 Chronicles 16:29
26. Robert L. Thomas, ed., *New American Standard Exhaustive Concordance of the Bible with Hebrew-Aramaic and Greek Dictionaries* (Nashville: Holman, 1981), 1640.
27. Hebrews 1:2
28. Hebrews 1:3
29. Thomas, *New American Standard Concordance,* 1662.
30. Isaiah 55:12
31. Simon Sebag Montefiore, *Jerusalem: The Biography* (New York: Knopf, 2011), 104.
32. Matthew Henry, *Matthew Henry's Commentary on the Whole Bible* (Peabody, MA: Hendrickson, 1991), 5:638.
33. Montefiore, *Jerusalem,* 104.
34. John 9:1–7
35. Montefiore, *Jerusalem,* 105–6.
36. John 1:46
37. Luke 2:41
38. Walter L. Liefeld, "Luke," in *The Expositor's Bible Commentary,* ed. Frank E. Gaebelein (Grand Rapids: Zondervan, 1992), 8:852.
39. Luke 2:49
40. Luke 2:49
41. Luke 2:50
42. Carolyn Custis James, *Lost Women of the Bible: Finding Strength and Significance Through Their Stories* (Grand Rapids: Zondervan, 2005), 171.
43. Luke 2:51
44. Montefiore, *Jerusalem,* 104.
45. Montefiore, *Jerusalem,* 106.
46. Isaiah 56:7, TLB
47. Jeremiah 7:11, NLT

Chapter 5: O Most Afflicted!

1. Matthew 21:21
2. Luke 20:5, MSG
3. Luke 20:6
4. Luke 20:7
5. Luke 20:8, NLT
6. *The Expanded Bible: Explore the Depths of the Scriptures While You Read* (Nashville: Thomas Nelson, 2011), note on Luke 21:1.
7. Robert L. Thomas, ed., *New American Standard Exhaustive Concordance of the Bible with Hebrew-Aramaic and Greek Dictionaries* (Nashville: Holman, 1981), 1663.
8. Thomas, *New American Standard Concordance,* 1635.
9. Matthew 26:15
10. Exodus 12:19
11. 1 Corinthians 5:8
12. John 6:35
13. Luke 22:7, NLV
14. 1 Corinthians 5:7
15. "Passover: The Seder Service in a Nutshell," Chabad.org, www.chabad.org/holidays/passover/pesach_cdo/aid/1751/jewish/The-Seder-in-a-Nutshell.htm.
16. Hebrews 13:8
17. Exodus 12:8
18. Walter L. Liefeld, "Luke," in *The Expositor's Bible Commentary,* ed. Frank E. Gaebelein (Grand Rapids: Zondervan, 1992), 8:1025.
19. Liefeld, "Luke," 8:1025.
20. Thomas, *New American Standard Concordance,* 1683.
21. Matthew 21:8
22. Adam Hamilton, *24 Hours That Changed the World* (Nashville: Abingdon, 2009), 18.
23. Miriam Feinberg Vamosh, *Women at the Time of the Bible* (Herzlia, Israel: Palphot, 2008), 86.
24. *The Expanded Bible,* note on Matthew 26:20.
25. John 13:1, TLB

26. Thomas, *New American Standard Concordance,* 1644.
27. *The Expanded Bible,* note on John 13:5.
28. Luke 9:18
29. Luke 9:20
30. Jeremiah 17:9
31. Jeremiah 17:10
32. Matthew 26:26
33. Matthew 26:27
34. *The Expanded Bible,* note on Matthew 26:30.
35. D. A. Carson, "Matthew," in *The Expositor's Bible Commentary,* ed. Frank E. Gaebelein (Grand Rapids: Zondervan, 1992), 8:539.
36. Thomas, *New American Standard Concordance,* 1682.
37. Zechariah 13:7
38. Isaiah 53:10, NASB
39. Matthew 16:18
40. Thomas, *New American Standard Concordance,* 1639.
41. Hamilton, *24 Hours That Changed the World,* 31.
42. Luke 22:41
43. Job 21:20
44. Matthew 26:41
45. Matthew 26:46
46. Matthew 26:47
47. Matthew 26:49
48. Matthew 26:50
49. Thomas, *New American Standard Concordance,* 1652.
50. Luke 22:53
51. Matthew 26:56
52. Frederick Dale Bruner, *The Gospel of John: A Commentary* (Grand Rapids: Eerdmans, 2012), 1107.

Chapter 6: Thorns Thine Only Crown

1. Luke 2:34
2. Luke 2:35
3. *The Expanded Bible: Explore the Depths of the Scriptures While You Read* (Nashville: Nelson, 2011), note on John 2:4.
4. "John 2:4," Bible Hub, http://biblehub.com/text/john/2-4.htm.

5. Edwyn Clement Hoskyns, *The Fourth Gospel,* ed. Francis Noel Davey, rev. 2nd ed. (London: Faber and Faber, 1947), 186.

6. Mark 10:7

7. Revelation 19:7

8. Frederick Dale Bruner, *The Gospel of John: A Commentary* (Grand Rapids: Eerdmans, 2012), 128.

9. Luke 2:35, CEB

10. John 8:44–45

11. Exodus 20:16

12. John 2:19

13. John 6:35

14. John 8:12

15. John 10:14

16. Robert L. Thomas, ed., *New American Standard Exhaustive Concordance of the Bible with Hebrew-Aramaic and Greek Dictionaries* (Nashville: Holman, 1981), 1645.

17. Luke 9:23

18. Luke 18:32

19. Thomas, *New American Standard Concordance,* 1680.

20. 1 Corinthians 6:20

21. Matthew 26:34

22. Matthew 26:69–70

23. Matthew 26:71–72

24. Matthew 26:74

25. Matthew 26:75

26. Luke 22:66

27. Luke 23:1

28. Luke 23:4

29. Luke 23:7

30. Luke 23:8–11

31. Luke 23:15

32. Luke 23:16

33. Luke 23:18

34. Luke 23:19

35. Richard D. Patterson, "The Use of Three in the Bible," Bible.org, February 26, 2008, http://bible.org/seriespage/3-use-three-bible.

36. Ephesians 5:2

37. *The Expanded Bible,* note on Mark 15:16.
38. Frances Vander Velde, *Women of the Bible* (Grand Rapids: Kregel, 1985), 179.
39. John 3:16
40. John 19:17
41. Hosea 10:8
42. Adam Hamilton, *24 Hours That Changed the World* (Nashville: Abingdon, 2009), 96.
43. Thomas, *New American Standard Concordance,* 1647.
44. John 19:23
45. John 19:23
46. John 19:24; Psalm 22:18
47. Thomas, *New American Standard Concordance,* 1646.
48. John 19:19
49. John 19:21
50. John 19:22
51. "Luke 23:42," Bible Hub, http://biblehub.com/text/luke /23-42.htm.

Chapter 7: At the Cross Her Station Keeping

1. 2 Samuel 18:33
2. E. P. Blair, "Salome," in *The Interpreter's Dictionary of the Bible: An Illustrated Encyclopedia,* ed. George Arthur Buttrick (Nashville: Abingdon, 1962), 4:167.
3. 1 Corinthians 15:58
4. Frederick Dale Bruner, *The Gospel of John: A Commentary* (Grand Rapids: Eerdmans, 2012), 1107.
5. Robert L. Thomas, ed., *New American Standard Exhaustive Concordance of the Bible with Hebrew-Aramaic and Greek Dictionaries* (Nashville: Holman, 1981), 1655.
6. Matthew 8:16
7. Thomas, *New American Standard Concordance,* 1664.
8. Rose Sallberg Kam, *Their Stories, Our Stories: Women of the Bible* (New York: Continuum, 1995), 220.
9. Susanne Heine, *Women and Early Christianity: A Reappraisal,* trans. John Bowden (Minneapolis: Augsburg, 1988), 77.

10. Adam Hamilton, *24 Hours That Changed the World* (Nashville: Abingdon, 2009), 99.

11. D. A. Carson, "Matthew," in *The Expositor's Bible Commentary,* ed. Frank E. Gaebelein (Grand Rapids: Zondervan, 1992), 8:583.

12. Thomas, *New American Standard Concordance,* 1640.

13. Matthew 12:48–50

14. Eli Lizorkin-Eyzenberg, *The Jewish Gospel of John: Discovering Jesus, King of All Israel* (Tel Aviv, Israel: Jewish Studies for Christians, 2015), 265.

15. Exodus 10:22

16. Carson, "Matthew," 8:578.

17. Matthew 4:1

18. Ephesians 6:12, KJV

19. Psalm 22:1

20. "Matthew 27:46," Bible Hub, http://biblehub.com/text /matthew/27-46.htm.

21. Matthew Henry, *Matthew Henry's Commentary on the Whole Bible* (Peabody, MA: Hendrickson, 1991), 5:347.

22. Psalm 69:21, NASB

23. Thomas, *New American Standard Concordance,* 1687.

24. Hebrews 9:7

25. Carson, "Matthew," 8:580.

26. Henry, *Matthew Henry's Commentary,* 5:349.

27. 1 Corinthians 12:3

28. Luke 23:48, AMPC

29. Hamilton, *24 Hours That Changed the World,* 96.

30. See Kenneth Barker, ed., *The NIV Study Bible: New International Version* (Grand Rapids: Zondervan, 1985), note on Mark 15:40.

31. Carson, "Matthew," 8:584.

32. Psalm 34:20

33. Isaac Watts, "When I Survey the Wondrous Cross," Hymnary. org, www.hymnary.org/text/when_i_survey_the_wondrous _cross_watts.

34. Zechariah 12:10

35. Mark 15:43
36. Carson, "Matthew," 8:584.
37. Mark 15:43
38. John 7:50
39. Carson, "Matthew," 8:584.
40. Alexander Moody Stuart, *The Three Marys: Mary of Magdala, Mary of Bethany, Mary of Nazareth* (Edinburgh, Scotland: Banner of Truth, 1984), 307.

Chapter 8: I Know That My Redeemer Lives

1. John 20:1
2. Mark 16:1
3. Luke 23:55
4. Luke 24:1
5. Matthew 28:1, GNV
6. John 20:1
7. Matthew 27:51–52
8. Matthew 28:5, MSG
9. John 4:28
10. 1 Peter 3:15, NLT
11. Luke 24:12
12. 1 John 4:19
13. Robert L. Thomas, ed., *New American Standard Exhaustive Concordance of the Bible with Hebrew-Aramaic and Greek Dictionaries* (Nashville: Holman, 1981), 1683.
14. Thomas, *New American Standard Concordance,* 1630.
15. Matthew 28:16–20
16. "John 20:17," Bible Hub, http://biblehub.com/text/john/20-17.htm.
17. Isaiah 6:8
18. Job 19:25
19. Luke 24:16
20. Luke 24:19
21. Luke 24:21
22. "1839. existémi," Bible Hub, http://biblehub.com/greek/1839.htm.

23. Luke 24:30–31
24. Luke 24:38–39
25. Luke 24:45
26. D. A. Carson, "Matthew," in *The Expositor's Bible Commentary,* ed. Frank E. Gaebelein (Grand Rapids: Zondervan, 1992), 8:581–82.
27. Thomas, *New American Standard Concordance,* 1648.
28. Matthew Henry, *Matthew Henry's Commentary on the Whole Bible* (Peabody, MA: Hendrickson, 1991), 5:350.
29. Ecclesiastes 8:17, GNT
30. Acts 1:3
31. Luke 24:50
32. Acts 1:5
33. Acts 1:9
34. Ephesians 4:4–6
35. Acts 1:13
36. Acts 1:14
37. Mark 16:7

Study Guide

1. "Abraham Joshua Heschel," Wikiquote, http://en.wikiquote.org /wiki/Abraham_Joshua_Heschel.
2. Frederick Dale Bruner, *The Gospel of John: A Commentary* (Grand Rapids: Eerdmans, 2012), 673.
3. Luke 10:41
4. Luke 10:42
5. Psalm 27:4, KJV
6. Brother Lawrence, *The Practice of the Presence of God* (New Kensington, PA: Whitaker House, 1982), 69.
7. John 11:5
8. John 11:27
9. Matthew 16:15
10. Matthew 16:16
11. Matthew 16:17
12. John 11:21, 32
13. John 11:33

14. John 11:35
15. John 11:25
16. Dolores Kimball, *Memorial: The Mystery of Mary of Bethany* (Darlington, UK: EP Books, 2014), 5.
17. Luke 7:28
18. Matthew 8:10
19. Matthew 15:28
20. Matthew 26:13
21. Mark 14:8, ojb
22. Luke 19:37
23. Matthew 21:9
24. Psalm 7:11
25. Lamentations 3:22–23
26. John 13:7
27. Matthew 26:45
28. Luke 23:27
29. Matthew Henry, *Matthew Henry's Commentary on the Whole Bible* (Peabody, MA: Hendrickson, 1991), 5:664.
30. Psalm 22:1
31. Psalm 22:19
32. John 19:25
33. Bruner, *The Gospel of John,* 1156.

Additional Bible Versions

Heartfelt Thanks

The Women of Easter began as an online Bible study during the Lenten season. What a joy it's been to gather all those words and many more between the covers of this book.

I treasure the thousands of sisters (and brothers) in Christ who faithfully read my monthly Bible study posts, and I'm especially thankful for their comments online. You've met some of these honest souls in our study guide: Amy, Nicole, Janice, Deb, Bonnie, Charlotte, Burqaj, Dana, and Tiffany. Thank you, sisters, for generously sharing your words with us. To join them and receive my free monthly Bible study in your e-mail inbox, visit www.LizCurtisHiggs.com/blog/ to subscribe. Your first name, your e-mail, and you're in!

Huge thanks to my editorial team, who waited and waited *and waited* as each chapter took shape: Laura Barker, Carol Bartley, Sara Fortenberry, Rebecca Price, Bill Higgs, Matthew Higgs, and Glenna Salsbury. I am ever in your debt. Again. Still.

Finally, big hugs to our proofreaders—Holly Briscoe, Alison Imbriaco, and Rachel Kirsch—our typesetter, Angie Messinger, and to Kelly Howard for another beautiful cover. I'm truly grateful for all the hands that touched this book.

Most of all, I'm grateful for *you,* my friend.

About the Author

Liz Curtis Higgs has one goal: to help women embrace the grace of God with joy and abandon. She is the author of more than thirty books, with 4.6 million copies in print, including *The Women of Christmas, It's Good to Be Queen, The Girl's Still Got It,* and *31 Verses to Write on Your Heart.*

In her million-selling Bad Girls of the Bible series, Liz breathes new life into ancient tales about the most famous women in scriptural history, from Eve to Jezebel to Delilah. Her award-winning historical novels, which transport the stories of Rebekah, Leah, Rachel, Dinah, Naomi, and Ruth to eighteenth-century Scotland, also invite readers to view biblical characters in a new light.

A seasoned professional speaker and Bible study teacher, Liz has toured with Women of Faith, Women of Joy, and Extraordinary Women. She has spoken for 1,700 women's conferences in all fifty states in the U.S. and fifteen foreign countries around the globe.

On the personal side, Liz is married to author Bill Higgs, PhD, who serves as director of operations for her speaking and writing office. Louisville is home for Liz and Bill, their grown children, and a delightful collection of cats.

Liz loves to connect with readers and friends on www .Facebook.com/LizCurtisHiggs, on www.Twitter.com/LizCurtis Higgs, on www.Vimeo.com/LizCurtisHiggs, and on www .Pinterest.com/LizCurtisHiggs.